THE VOYAGE TO ILLYRIA

A New Study of Shakespeare

THE VOYAGE
TO ILLYRIA

A New Study of Shakespeare

KENNETH MUIR
SEAN O'LOUGHLIN

*The road to Xanadu could not be more
phantom-thronged than the voyage to
Illyria.*   A. L. ATTWATER

BARNES & NOBLE, Inc.
New York
METHUEN & CO. Ltd
London

First published, 1937

This edition reprinted, 1970
by Barnes & Noble, Inc.
and Methuen & Co. Ltd.

Barnes & Noble ISBN 389 04052 5

Methuen ISBN 416 17400 0

Printed in the United States of America

PREFACE

The Voyage to Illyria originated in a correspondence between the two authors soon after they graduated some forty years ago. It was finished in 1936 and published in the following year. Between then and now my views on Shakespeare have undergone a change. They are now less positive and more sceptical, more cautious and less romantic; but since the book gets listed in bibliographies and occasionally quoted, I welcome the chance of seeing it once more in print.

We have had to leave the text unaltered; and, as Sean O'Loughlin and I no longer agree, this preface expresses only my views. I would not now attempt to construct a biography from the evidence provided by a dramatist's works; I am less certain than I was about the identity of Mr. W.H., nor do I think it greatly matters; and I do not suppose that Shakespeare's 'mythical sorrows' (as Professor C. J. Sisson called them) were the cause of his tragic period. My present views on Shakespeare are available in several books and articles. But I would still accept Keats's remark that Shakespeare led a life of allegory, his works being the comments on it, even though I would not relate this spiritual biography to the actual events of his life. This, I think, is my main point of disagreement with my fellow author. Re-reading the book after more than thirty years, it seems to me less important as a biography than for its incidental criticism, much of which I still believe to be valid.

University of Liverpool   KENNETH MUIR

The authors make their grateful acknowledgments to the editors of *The Dublin Magazine* and of *The Times Literary Supplement* for permission to reprint portions of this book which have appeared in their columns.

CONTENTS

I

THE APPROACH

*Shakespeare is the only biographer of Shakespeare. . . .
So far from Shakespeare's being the least known, he is
the one person in all modern history fully known to us.*

R. W. EMERSON

I

IF the aim of Shakespearean criticism be justice, the plays of Shakespeare must eventually be studied by comparison with each other, no longer as separate entities. They must be related to one another, to the poems, and to the *Sonnets*. Each individual play acquires a deeper significance from its setting in the corpus. Too often the type of criticism that views each play in isolation proclaims that *Troilus and Cressida*, *Measure for Measure*, even *Hamlet*, are failures ; that *King Lear* is not suitable for acting ; and that *Cymbeline* was fitted with a happy ending to suit the fashion set by Beaumont and Fletcher. If we are enabled to judge these plays by reference to a single criterion, our effort will not have been in vain.

That criterion is to be sought in the personality of the poet, and this will be our concern. We have no quarrel with those who refuse to occupy themselves with the poet's personality, and we sympathize with many of their criticisms of the opposite school, but a misapplication of good methods does not automatically invalidate the theory on which they rest. Our starting-point has been admirably defined by Sir Edmund Chambers in his defence of the authenticity of the canon :

After all, we have read the plays for ourselves, and have learnt to recognize in them, through all their diversities, a continuous personality, of which style is only one aspect. A single mind and a single hand dominate them. They are the outcome of one man's critical reactions to life,

3

which make the stuff of comedy, and of one man's emotional reactions to life, which make the stuff of tragedy.

And we put forward this book as a reasoned attempt to convince the sceptical of the validity of the personal heresy. It is only too evident, from a study of Shakespearean criticism, that the portrait of the poet which emerges is more often a self-portrait of the critic. We hope to have minimized that danger by our consciousness of its existence, and by the method of collaboration. Though we are, of course, indebted to many of our predecessors, we have also used, without slavishly accepting, the conclusions of modern psychology. We have endeavoured by its means to range the discoveries of Whiter, Miss Caroline Spurgeon, and Professor Wilson Knight in their just perspective, and, so far as we could, to bridge the gulf between the theories of Frank Harris and the self-denying scholarship of Sir Edmund Chambers. Any force the book may have is cumulative, and we beg the reader, therefore, to suspend judgment until the last page has been read.

It will at once be urged that such an attempt may succeed with a romantic poet, and yet fail miserably when applied to Shakespeare, who was, moreover, mainly a dramatic poet. 'Others abide our question. Thou art free.' But he was not so objective as Arnold (then twenty-five) would have us believe, and we must set out the various avenues of approach to the mystery which is Shakespeare. They are five :

1. His biography.
2. His changing attitude to certain obvious concepts.
3. False notes, recurrences, and fervours.

4. His use of imagery.
5. His use and treatment of his sources.

The first approach is the most important, since it is direct, and leaves little to inference. Had we the same wealth of material that we possess for later poets, letters, personal reminiscences, and biographies written while his close friends and his relations were still alive, the whole question would have been settled long ago. In Shakespeare's day, however, only the socially and politically great were considered worthy of commemoration, though Heywood planned, but apparently never wrote, his *Lives of all the Poets*. On the other hand, what we possess is of great assistance, and to it we have added the evidence of the *Sonnets*, which, after mature consideration, we see no reason to accept at other than their face value.

Under the heading 'His attitude to certain obvious concepts', we shall find most of our evidence. The poet concerns himself with emotional problems, and if he is to advance, he must face those problems. The record, then, of his solved problems is the record of his spiritual development, and when all problems have been solved, the impulse to write normally dies out. It is as if the Life Force, having employed the instrument for its purpose, cast it away, its task done. But several of the greatest artists have ended with a magical state, in which conflicts no longer arise. Only technical problems remain. It is then that their greatest and serenest works are produced. The romantic becomes classical, but on a plane where such labels are meaningless.

This development is closely connected with certain quite natural problems of human life, and with their solution. Death is one problem that every man must face, and the conquest of death and time is one of the aims of all artists, for 'Death comes equally to us all, and makes us all equal when it comes'. The bitterness against faithless lovers arises because the faithless one, having sworn to be true for ever, thus defeating Time, finally proves Time's omnipotence, and the artist is himself defeated by the defeat of love. Poetry is 'a forted residence 'gainst the tooth of time And razure of oblivion'. Shakespeare, having in vain pleaded with his friend to marry, in order that his beauty should not be lost in the grave, declared that he would perpetuate it by his art. The plays may be regarded, from one important aspect, as a series of conquests over the fear of death, on successively higher levels, until in *The Tempest* he could depart in peace, having seen salvation, a salvation which emerged from his previous attempts, and could be attained to only when all his other problems had been solved. He had forgiven ; and death had no more power over him. The nature of the subsidiary problems will be made apparent when we come to discuss the separate plays.[1]

The third approach we have postulated is by means of false notes, recurrences, and fervours. We have not attempted an exhaustive treatment of these, since a so-called 'false note' may be claimed by another critic as part of Shakespeare's intention of holding the mirror up to Nature. Nevertheless, when the false notes recur, we are in a stronger position. When the poet reverts to seemingly irrelevant topics, it is justifiable to infer that, to him, the topic was not irrelevant.

This method of investigation is closely linked with a

[1] See Appendix.

study of the poet's imagery. Metaphor and simile are part of Shakespeare's mental processes. His thought moved by images, and his utterance was conditioned by the sequence that the association of ideas provoked. He embroidered his main theme with a counterpoint of imagery that sprang from his unconscious mind, and whatever the objectivity of the actual words spoken, the imagery betrays the attitude of the dramatist. Images are to the poet what inflexions of the voice are to the speaker. The first use of the method was by Walter Whiter in a book published in 1794, entitled *A Specimen of a Commentary on Shakespeare . . . on a new principle of criticism derived from Mr. Locke's Doctrine of the Association of Ideas.* This is in every way a remarkable piece of work, anticipating by more than a century some of the most interesting discoveries of the past dozen years, though nobody, so far, has attempted to draw any biographical inferences from the material provided by such investigations. By this means, we are enabled to discover the successive problems that beset Shakespeare, and the theme of our book is a description of the journey that the poet visualized in his most persistent and vital imagery, and a recognition of the pregnant saying of Keats that ' Shakespeare led a life of Allegory. His works are the comments on it '.

Our last consideration is the treatment of the sources from which Shakespeare derived the crude material for his plays. In a considerable number of instances he altered very little. This may be due to one of two causes. The material may have been exactly suited to his requirements, or he may have been too weary or too bored to make any alteration. In each case, we must judge the problem on its merits. When he made alterations, their form and reason must weigh very considerably in our judgment of the genesis of his play. What he omits, inserts, or simply expands will often furnish a clue, and we have found such evidence of considerable value as a confirmation of other methods of approach, and as a pointer to an explanation of some of the more enigmatic plays ; for instance, *Measure for Measure.*

We have devoted our second chapter to an examination of the effect of external events on Shakespeare's mind, and the third and fourth to an analysis of their reaction on his art. Thenceforward, we have endeavoured to show how, with his triumphant emergence as a complete master of dramatic poetry, he ceased to write light-hearted comedy, why that change coincided with the appearance of the great tragedies, and why, finally, he abandoned tragedy to write romance.

II

THE KEY

With this key
Shakspere unlocked his heart.

WORDSWORTH

II

HAVING sketched out the method of approach, we must now apply it, and review the material we possess for a study of Shakespeare. Of his private letters we lack even the least scrap. Even of his handwriting we have no more than a few signatures, to his will and to business documents, and a page or so of a dramatic MS. showing him at work, cobbling a play that failed to meet with the approval of the licensing authorities.

But the rest is not silence. Industrious and tireless research has brought to light innumerable fragments of his career, and enabled us to decide the date of composition of his plays with an accuracy that was inconceivable a hundred years ago. Sir Edmund Chambers's masterly two volumes contain the essence of all that is known, and it is on this foundation of unassailable fact that the ensuing structure of hypothesis has been erected. It is true, we believe, that on no occasion have we been called on to dispute or evade any positive assertion made by him, and even in the case of the name of the fair youth of the *Sonnets* (though identifications are of value to us only as convenient pegs), we are in agreement with Sir Edmund's views as expressed in the last edition of the *Encyclopædia Britannica*.

Any species of hypothesis that starts from Baconian or Oxfordian premises can proceed only by the fatal advance of *ignotum per ignotius*. We have accepted the facts as they stand, and, if we are accused of taking them too much at their face value, our only reply is the simple one, that in that case, and that case alone, do the facts cease to be contradictory. The onus of proof rests with the other side.

Let us examine the situation as we find it in 1593 and 1594. William Shakespeare, who was born in April 1564, the son of respectable but not wealthy parents, was beginning to make a modest reputation for himself in London. In 1592, Robert Greene, on his death-bed, had denounced him as a danger to the playwrights of the time, an actor without a university education, successfully imitating the works of his social and intellectual superiors. Henry Chettle, Greene's literary executor, however, was constrained in the same year to modify the onslaught, and to confess that Shakespeare had been maligned :

My selfe haue seene his demeanor no lesse ciuill than he exelent in the qualitie he professes : Besides, diuers of worship haue reported his vprightnes of dealing, which argues his honesty, and his featious grace in writting, which aprooues his Art.

In the following year, 1593, was published a poem entitled *Venus and Adonis*, dedicated to the young Henry Wriothesley, then twenty years of age, ' Earle of Southampton, and Baron of Titchfield '. The dedication ran thus :

Right Honourable, I know not how I shall offend in dedicating my vnpolisht lines to your Lordship, nor how the worlde vvil censure mee for choosing so strong a proppe to support so vveake a burthen, onelye if your Honour seeme but pleased, I account my selfe highly praised, and vowe to take aduantage of all idle houres, till I haue honoured you vvith some grauer labour. But if the first

heire of my inuention proue deformed, I shall be sorie it
had so noble a god-father : and neuer after eare so barren
a land, for feare it yeeld me still so bad a haruest, I leaue
it to your Honourable suruey, and your Honor to your
hearts content, vvhich I wish may alvvaies ansvvere your
ovvne vvish, and the vvorldes hopefull expectation.

Your Honors in all dutie,

WILLIAM SHAKESPEARE

Within a year the promise of ' some grauer labour ' was
fulfilled, and in 1594, *Lucrece* appeared, dedicated to the
same great lord thus :

The loue I dedicate to your Lordship is without end :
wherof this Pamphlet without beginning is but a super-
fluous Moity. The warrant I haue of your Honourable
disposition, not the worth of my vntutord Lines makes it
assured of acceptance. VVhat I haue done is yours, what
I haue to doe is yours, being part in all I haue, deuoted yours.
VVere my worth greater, my duety would shew greater,
meane time, as it is, it is bound to your Lordship ; to
whom I wish long life still lengthned with all happinesse.

Your Lordships in all duety.

WILLIAM SHAKESPEARE

Coming from an age when fulsomeness was the fashion,
and servility the passport to favour, such language is
usually taken as a typical specimen of Elizabethan adulation.
Let us see, however, what Professor Nichol Smith says on
the subject of the dedication of *Lucrece* in an essay contributed to *Shakespeare's England*, and entitled ' Authors and
Patrons ' :

13

THE VOYAGE TO ILLYRIA

The difference in tone in the dedications of *Venus and Adonis* and *The Rape of Lucrece* is remarkable. Aloof and formal terms give place, within a year, to expressions of affection whose like will not easily be found. . . . There is no other dedication like this in Elizabethan literature. As *The Rape of Lucrece* was the last book that Shakespeare published, he did not again have occasion to speak of Southampton by name, and further proofs of their friendship must be sought in the *Sonnets*.

In 1609 a book was issued for the (now) modest sum of fivepence, entitled *Shakes-peares Sonnets. Neuer before Imprinted.* That, however, is not the first indication we have of their existence. As long before as 1598, Francis Meres, a Rutland clergyman, in his *Palladis Tamia*, a solemn collection of Elizabethan literary anecdotes with a leaning towards antithesis and moralizing, had concluded his remarks on Shakespeare's poetical works with a reference to his ' sugred Sonnets among his priuate friends, &c.' The following year witnessed the publication of a collection of verse under the title of *The Passionate Pilgrim*, ' By W. Shakespeare '. This contained pieces attributed to Shakespeare—wrongly in some cases. The third edition, 1612, appears in one copy with the name of Shakespeare removed from the title-page, and what was evident from this, Heywood, in 1612, had already made known, that Shakespeare resented the attribution to him of other men's work, and, if Heywood is to be believed, Shakespeare actually caused his own volume of sonnets to be published in authentic form, as Heywood says, ' to doe himselfe right '. But there were, in *The Passionate Pilgrim* of 1599, some things indubitably Shakespeare's. Some had already appeared in *Love's Labour's Lost* the previous year, and two sonnets reappeared, in a revised (and embittered) form, in the collected volume of 1609. It would seem that no further edition of the Sonnets appeared in Shakespeare's lifetime, nor, for a long time, were they to appear again in their original guise. In 1640, notwithstanding, a new edition came out, with a prefatory avowal by the publisher, John Benson, to the reader :

I Here presume (under favour) to present to your view, some excellent and sweetely composed Poems, of Master *William Shakespeare*, Which in themselves appeare of the same purity, the Authour him-selfe then living avouched.

The changes introduced were more misleading than actually lying, but they seem to reflect the views of the period on the propriety of some of the sonnets. The headings emphasize, in a considerable number of cases, the sex of the recipient as feminine, whereas, from the poems themselves, we can see this is patently wrong, and, moreover, the order is so changed as to disguise any sequence which may originally have been of crucial importance.

Thenceforward, until the end of the eighteenth century, the study of Shakespeare the Dramatist overshadowed the study of Shakespeare the Poet and Shakespeare the Man. Eccentric Steevens even went so far as to say that not even an Act of Parliament could persuade people to read such sorry stuff as the *Sonnets*. But there were indications of a change of attitude, and a closer study of the *Sonnets* produced an immediate result. It was observed that many of them were addressed to a young man in terms more usually employed in addressing a woman, and thus was raised again the problem which the editor of 1640 had set himself fairly successfully to obscure.

Let us summarize now, as briefly as possible, the prima facie intention of the *Sonnets*, as they were originally put forth in 1609. There are two groups, the first of 126 sonnets, the ultimate one of which, in twelve lines, seems to be an *envoi* to the set, and the rest, with the exception of two based on a fifth-century Greek epigram of Marianus Scholasticus, found in the *Palatine Anthology*, constitute a second group, 'a disordered appendix'. These two groups dovetail by fairly obvious links, though they are not addressed to the same person ; and it is axiomatic that these two sets, as they stand, make a coherent and strictly relevant whole, requiring no re-arrangement. The first seventeen sonnets coincide in intention and theme with *Venus and Adonis*, and there are a considerable number of verbal echoes. The poet's plea to the youth to whom this group is addressed, to marry in order to perpetuate his beauty, is the argument Venus employs to persuade Adonis. In *Sonnet* 18, Shakespeare declares his deep affection for the young man, and we hear no more of marriage pleas. Now, he boasts that the lovely boy is immortalized in his verse :

So long as men can breath or eyes can see,
So long liues this, and this giues life to thee.

Sonnet 20 is an unequivocal declaration of love, and, in the next sonnet, comes the first hint of a rival, whose name, from the punning and oblique reference in *Love's Labour's Lost* to 'base sale of chapmens tongues', seems

THE KEY

fairly evident. Furthermore, the same sonnet gives a clue by its contents :

So is it not with me as with that Muse,
Stird by a painted beauty to his verse,
Who heauen it selfe for ornament doth vse,
And euery faire with his faire doth reherse,
Making a coopelment of proud compare
With Sunne and Moone, with earth and seas rich gems :
With Aprills first borne flowers and all things rare,
That heauens ayre in this huge rondure hems.

Unfortunately the poem cannot be traced in Chapman's work, and the problem still remains.

Sonnet 26 accompanied *Lucrece*, and is a poetical version of the prose dedication already quoted above :

Lord of my loue, to whome in vassalage
Thy merrit hath my dutie strongly knit ;
To thee I send this written ambassage
To witnesse duty, not to shew my wit.
Duty so great, which wit so poore as mine
May make seeme bare, in wanting words to shew it ;
But that I hope some good conceipt of thine
In thy soules thought (all naked) will bestow it :
Til whatsoeuer star that guides my mouing,
Points on me gratiously with faire aspect,
And puts apparrell on my tottered louing,
To show me worthy of thy sweet respect,
    Then may I dare to boast how I doe loue thee,
    Till then, not show my head where thou maist proue me.

THE VOYAGE TO ILLYRIA

The resemblances are too clear to need underlining.
The dedication is echoed in *Sonnets* 32, 37, 39 and 54. In
the group 33–42, the poet complains that his mistress
has seduced his friend. In these, some of the finest poetry
of the earlier Shakespeare is to be found, notably in 33:

Full many a glorious morning haue I seene,
Flatter the mountaine tops with soueraine eie,
Kissing with golden face the meddowes greene ;
Guilding pale streames with heauenly alcumy :
Anon permit the basest cloudes to ride,
With ougly rack on his celestiall face,
And from the for-lorne world his visage hide
Stealing vnseene to west with this disgrace :
Euen so my Sunne one early morne did shine,
With all triumphant splendor on my brow,
But out alack, he was but one houre mine,
The region cloude hath mask'd him from me now.
　　Yet him for this, my loue no whit disdaineth,
　　Suns of the world may staine, when heauens sun staineth.

Capable of such detachment, the poet resigned mistress
to friend, and wrote of it thus :

　　Take all my loues, my loue, yea take them all,
　　What hast thou then more then thou hadst before ?
　　No loue, my loue, that thou maist true loue call,
　　All mine was thine, before thou hadst this more :
　　Then if for my loue, thou my loue receiuest,
　　I cannot blame thee, for my loue thou vsest,
　　But yet be blam'd, if thou this self deceauest
　　By wilfull taste of what thy selfe refusest.

18

THE KEY

I doe forgiue thy robb'rie gentle theefe
Although thou steale thee all my pouerty :
And yet loue knowes it is a greater griefe
To beare loues wrong, then hates knowne iniury.
Lasciuious grace in whom all il wel showes,
Kill me with spights yet we must not be foes.

But the sonnets addressed to the mistress who caused this calamity are less self-possessed. In 133 to 144, the theme is again treated, but with a bitterness of reproach aimed at the guilty party. This is what the poet says in *Sonnet* 144 :

Two loues I haue of comfort and dispaire,
Which like two spirits do sugiest me still,
The better angell is a man right faire :
The worser spirit a woman collour'd il.
To win me soone to hell my female euill,
Tempteth my better angel from my sight,
And would corrupt my saint to be a diuel :
Wooing his purity with her fowle pride.
And whether that my angel be turn'd fiend,
Suspect I may, yet not directly tell,
But being both from me both to each friend,
gesse one angel in an others hel.
Yet this shal I nere know but liue in doubt,
Till my bad angel fire my good one out.

It is clear, from many of Shakespeare's utterances, for example *Sonnets* 87, 88, and 93, that his friendship had been returned, though in a rather superficial measure, but he began to fear, more and more, that there was a coolness that boded ill (87–93). He makes so bold as to admonish his friend for lascivious conduct (94–96), and an interval is evident between 96 and 97 ('How like a Winter hath my absence been'), and 104 reveals the passage of three years since their first meeting :

> Three Winters colde,
> Haue from the forrests shooke three summers pride,
> Three beautious springs to yellow *Autumne* turn'd,
> In processe of the seasons haue I seene;
> Three Aprill perfumes in three hot Iunes burn'd,
> Since first I saw you fresh which yet are greene.

If we assume that the first sonnets are part of the same inspiration that produced *Venus and Adonis*, we may date 104 as 1596–7. In the next group, the poet admits some fault of his own, and blames his profession as the cause, 'the publicke meanes which publicke manners breeds'. He pleads that he has 'frequent binne with vnknowne mindes' to test the constancy of love, and his most moving utterance, 'Let me not to the marriage of true mindes,' is an assertion of his fundamental loyalty. But something irrevocable has come to pass. The most feeling asseverations appear to be bolstering up a failing faith, and in the envoi he goes back on his promise of immortality :

> O Thou my louely Boy who in thy power,
> Doest hould times fickle glasse, his sickle-hower :
> Who hast by wayning growne, and therein shou'st,
> Thy louers withering, as thy sweet selfe grow'st.
> If Nature (soueraine misteres ouer wrack)

THE KEY

As thou goest onwards still will plucke thee backe,
She keepes thee to this purpose, that her skill
May time disgrace, and wretched mynuit kill.
Yet feare her O thou minnion of her pleasure,
She may detaine, but not still keepe her tresure !
Her *Audite* (though delayd) answer'd must be,
And her *Quietus* is to render thee.

The change of tone in this poem is full of significance.
It marks an end to the beliefs expressed in the preceding
sonnets. Any feeling of permanence that the friendship had
engendered was gone, and into the maw of Time all was
to go, all . . . save the recollection of what had been, and
what might have been. When Heminges and Condell
dedicated the First Folio, they turned to 'the most noble
and incomparable paire of brethren', the Earls of Pembroke
and Montgomery. Such, in brief, is what has justly been
called, though perhaps without a full realization of its
implications, 'the drama of the *Sonnets*'.

Let us turn now to a piece of sixteenth century scandal
published in the latter part of 1594 under the title of
Willobie His Avisa. It treats of the assaults made by three
separate persons on the chastity of a virtuous wife Avisa,
recounted in poetical epistles between the parties concerned.
The portion that invites our attention begins at Canto
XLIII. There is a preliminary note thus :

Henrico Willobego.   Italo-Hispalensis.
H.W. being sodenly infected with the contagion of a
fantasticall fit, at the first sight of *A*, pyneth a while in
secret griefe, at length not able any longer to indure the
burning heate of so feruent a humour, bewrayeth the secresy

21

of his disease vnto his familiar frend W.S. who not long before had tryed the curtesy of the like passion, and was now newly recouered of the like infection ; yet finding his frend let bloud in the same vaine, he took pleasure for a tyme to see him bleed, & in steed of stopping the issue, he inlargeth the wound, with the sharpe rasor of a willing conceit, perswading him that he thought it a matter very easie to be compassed, & no doubt with payne, diligence & some cost in time to be obtayned. Thus this miserable comforter comforting his frend with an impossibilitie, eyther for that he now would secretly laugh at his frends folly, that had giuen occasion not long before vnto others to laugh at his owne, or because he would see whether an other could play his part better then himselfe, & in vewing a far off the course of this louing Comedy, he determined to see whether it would sort to a happier end for this new actor, then it did for the old player. But at length this Comedy was like to haue growen to a Tragedy, by the weake and feeble estate that H.W. was brought vnto . . .

In the verses which ensue, there is not much of special interest apart from a couplet in Canto XLVII, line 5 :

> She is no Saynt, She is no Nonne,
> I thinke in tyme she may be wonne

addressed by W. S. to H. W., and this bears a noticeable resemblance to *Titus Andronicus* II i 83 :

> Shee is a woman, therefore may be woo'd.
> Shee is a woman, therefore may be wonne,

and to *Richard III* I ii 229 :

> Was euer woman in this humour woo'd ?
> Was euer woman in this humour wonne ?

It is interesting to observe that in the *Apologie* to the
'1596' edition of *Willobie His Avisa* Hadrian Dorrell, in
his disclaimer of any personal satire intended by the author,
should say, in this connexion :

> Some others there be, who when they haue read this
> booke, haue blushed to themselues, finding, as they thought,
> their very words and writings which they had vsed in the
> like attempts.

Qui s'excuse, s'accuse. The book was suppressed. It seems
scarcely open to doubt that ' Henrico Willobego ' is Henry
Wriothesley, and that ' W. S. ' ' the old player ' is William
Shakespeare. Furthermore, in view of what we have
said with regard to the dating of the *Sonnets*, we have no
real doubt that the fair young man to whom most of them
were addressed, was Southampton also.

We may return now to the *Sonnets* themselves, and
endeavour to discover what had brought about this state of
affairs, and what were Shakespeare's reactions to the series
of events portrayed there. We must, first of all, rid our
minds of any presuppositions. A whole essay has been
written to demonstrate the normality of Shakespeare in
his treatment of love and marriage. It is an able and
scholarly study, but it is not the last word. We may take,
as a crucial instance, the following, where the evidence is

unimpugnable, and compare *Sonnet* 14, written to the fair young man :

Not from the stars do I my iudgement plucke . . .
But from thine eies my knowledge I deriue.

with *Love's Labour's Lost* IV iii 302.

From womens eyes this doctrine I deriue.

Here we have a real transference from the private to the public document, and the same process recurs frequently. It is not too much to say that this necessity of rectification must have aided Shakespeare to a notable extent in his dramatic composition, when his whole life was conditioned by the same necessity, and in this context, ' All the world's a stage ' acquires a deeper significance. But Shakespeare was perfectly conscious that all was not well, and to that extent he was normal. He made no pathetic defence of his aberration. Let us see what that aberration was.

Shakespeare, we know, was married to a woman considerably older than himself, Ann Hathaway. It has been surmised that she seduced him. The external evidence is slight. The entering of a bond is all we have to go on. Perhaps that is why we have Shylock. But this is fanciful; and Ann does not come into the picture, though we may suspect that some of Shakespeare's shrews are portraits from life. On the other hand, he was in bondage to the Dark Lady of the *Sonnets*. ' Bondage ' is the only word that fitly describes the situation. Love between them was no more than a ' sensuall feast'. The attachment offered nothing else. Moreover, it was adulterous on both sides :

THE KEY

But thou art twice forsworne to me loue swearing,
In act thy bed-vow broake,

and to this servitude he brought two compensations. He
rationalized his detestation of the woman he served by
asserting the impurity and inconstancy of her sex, and
strengthened it by reserving his affection for the fair young
man. Orthodox and prudish criticism strains at the gnat of
the fair young man to swallow the camel of the Dark
Lady. The notorious twentieth sonnet has caused a great
deal of heart-burning. Those who countenance it at all,
whether sympathetically or not, appear to be agreed on
its intentions. We must see it in full, since, in our
belief, *it* is the key with which Shakespeare unlocked his
heart :

A Womans face with natures owne hand painted,
Haste thou the Master Mistris of my passion,
A womans gentle hart but not acquainted
With shifting change as is false womens fashion,
An eye more bright then theirs, lesse false in rowling :
Gilding the obiect where-vpon it gazeth,
A man in hew all *Hews* in his controwling,
Which steales mens eyes and womens soules amaseth.
And for a woman wert thou first created,
Till nature as she wrought thee fell a dotinge,
And by addition me of thee defeated,
By adding one thing to my purpose nothing.
    But since she prickt thee out for womens pleasure,
    Mine be thy loue and thy loues vse their treasure.

Here we have the antithesis of ' false women ' and constant

men, but it is quite clear that the declaration is of innocent and Platonic love for the fair youth.

Nevertheless, such a state of affairs was bound to have its effect, and we see it in the poems. Broadly speaking, *Venus and Adonis* corresponds with the sonnets addressed to Southampton, and *Lucrece* with the group addressed to the ' dark lady '. Verbally and imagistically, as well as psychologically, these four groups are inseparably related. The influence on the plays, though not so striking at first glance, is even more profound, especially with regard to the female characters. Their unreality and doll-like character has been a matter for frequent comment. The bawds have the sex of women ; the heroines only the virtues. To plead that Shakespeare had in mind the limitations of the boy-actors who took the parts is irrelevant when we remember Cleopatra. At most, it is a fortunate accident.

Towards the turn of the century there is a plain falling-off in the quality of the plays, especially *King John* and *Henry V*. The pages which present the exposition of the ramifications of the Salic Law are among the dullest in the canon. Shakespeare was apparently growing weary of dramatic writing. But historical plays (into which the personality of the poet entered least) are on two occasions the prelude to a fresh development of his art. *Henry VI* and *Henry V* are the calms before the tempest. They presage *Titus Andronicus* and *Julius Caesar*. A wrench was evident in the latter play. It had as its fulcrum the character of Caesar. There is no historical character to whom Shakespeare made such frequent reference, and the dramatic identification is clear. The play's nucleus is betrayal, and its real counterpart is to be sought in the rupture which followed the last of the *Sonnets*. Shakespeare revealed, by a passing reference in *Henry V*, that he was already reading North's *Plutarch*, the source of *Julius Caesar*, and it would seem that the shock of betrayal numbed his imagination, and was re-acted soon after in *Julius Caesar*. It is Caesar's most trusted friend, his ' angel ' Brutus, who is responsible for the betrayal, and, furthermore, the theme of ingratitude pervades many of the succeeding plays, notably *As You Like It, King Lear*, and *Timon of Athens*. The rupture with Southampton now drives the poet to seek a fresh orientation. He is now forced to grapple with realities, and to cast away the hope of Platonic compromise. It is this spiritual journey that Shakespeare depicts in the plays of what people, by general consent, call his tragic period. There is a long period of Romantic disillusionment and bitterness, marked most clearly in *Hamlet* and *Troilus and Cressida*. He is still pursued by the ghost of the impurity and inconstancy of women. Hamlet's grievance is the Queen's disloyalty to her first husband, and in Ophelia purity and constancy are offered up on the altar of the poet's burning dramatic imagination in order to satisfy his disbelief in the virtue of women. Ophelia, Desdemona, Cordelia, all are swept down, Cordelia in defiance of the plot that Shakespeare had before him in the source-play, *King Leir*.

One of the reasons why *Measure for Measure* is such an unsatisfactory play probably lies in the fact that it was imperative that purity should suffer in the character of Isabella, but, since her suffering could, by the demands of the plot, be only at the expense of her purity, Shakespeare was at an impasse which could be avoided only by the clumsy device of Mariana of the moated grange. Here again, his treatment in the alteration of the plot of his source is noteworthy.

There can be no doubt whatever that between 1599 and 1605 the poet was rapidly coming down to essentials in an attempt to make the synthesis of sex and love which had been denied him all his life. *Macbeth*, as we can see from the imagery, which so profoundly recalls that of *Lucrece*, was a symbolical exploration of the theme of desire divorced from love. The hero's downfall reflects the author's dissatisfaction. The poet's approach to the problems of his own life is not through some form of Freudian analysis. His cry is ' to pluck from the memory a rooted sorrow ', Hamlet's avowal of revenge embodies the same desire to forget, and there is, all the time, the prayer for sleep or death to end it all. It is in *King Lear* that rock-bottom is reached. Not for nothing are the King's ravings of sex. It is to the universal law which affects even the gilded fly that Lear refuses to submit. In the imperfect *Timon of Athens*, we reach the centre of the Inferno, and here the poet's resistance broke.

With *Antony and Cleopatra*, the fusion of love and sex, with its consequent regeneration, is evident. Come to an age when he can find a true mate amongst womankind, and aided, no doubt, by the mellowing of his personality with the maturity of middle age, Shakespeare announces the long-sought synthesis in the perfect loyalty of a real woman, Cleopatra. *Antony and Cleopatra* answers to the true maturity of the poet's mind. No longer is he the unwilling bond-slave of the *Sonnets*. He is no longer obliged to take refuge in the belief that women are inconstant, and he is able, at last, to comprehend the sacrifice that such a woman as Cleopatra makes, because he can love her. It is evident that Stendhal's view of love as crystallization was Shakespeare's, since he made Cleopatra talk of a squeaking boy aping her greatness, and it is not without interest that the access of vitality which this new conquest gave him showed itself in a quite sudden advance in metrical technique towards the form of the Romances.

But the maturity, so long delayed, was not the end. If *Antony and Cleopatra* was the paean of love, the Romances of Shakespeare's last years were the testament. Here the purity of Marina, of Imogen, of Hermione, and of Miranda was to survive the dramatic stress, and, finally, Shakespeare, embodying his imagination as Prospero and his inspiration as Ariel, was content to abjure his rough magic, cast his book to the ocean-bottom, deeper than ever plummet sounded, and take leave of his audience with the request of merciful forgiveness. He had entered the kingdom of the full poetic consciousness. The wheel had again come full circle.

III

TUTELAGE

Part I

The prophetick soule,
Of the wide world, dreaming on things to come.

SONNET 107

III

IN 1582, Shakespeare married a woman eight years his senior, and the birth of a child five months later makes it natural to assume that he was compelled to do so, either by family pressure or by his own sense of duty. As Mr. Bernard Shaw has pointed out, Shakespeare's heroines take the initiative ; and from this and the evidence of *Venus and Adonis*, it is reasonable to suppose that Shakespeare was virtually seduced by Ann Hathaway. Adonis says to Venus :

> You do it for increase, ô straunge excuse !
> VVhen reason is the bawd to lusts abuse.

It would be a very strange excuse for Venus to employ, but for Ann a normal rationalization.

Can we discover anything about the personality of the boy of eighteen whose passion or curiosity made him fall a victim to the daughter of a neighbouring farmer, one day in the summer of 1582 ? Miss Caroline Spurgeon, from her study of the imagery of the poet, has drawn up a list of characteristics which must have been his, even in his youth, but it needed no special study to tell us that he was acutely observant, and sensitive both to the beautiful and ugly things of life, that he had, in short, the equipment of a poet.

It is in his relations with his family that the problem of interpretation is insoluble. No safe conclusions can be drawn from the records. That Shakespeare married a woman older than himself would be taken by the psychologists as a proof that he was seeking a mother-substitute, and, since Hamlet has been diagnosed as suffering from an Oedipus complex, it is only a small step to saddle his creator with one. But if such were the case, there would have been no play without patent traces of it. The evidence of the sonnets addressed to Southampton would naturally not conflict with this theory, but the evidence of his relationship with the Dark Lady is an obstacle, and the trouble does not appear to be as deeply rooted or so long-standing as a mother-fixation would imply. There was another reason, one to which due weight must first be given—the insulating effect of his own genius. To affix a label is not to explain, and all we can say is that our views do not conflict with a psycho-analytical interpretation, but that such an interpretation requires far more evidence than we have at our disposal.

With those who err on the other side by refusing to take the evidence of the *Sonnets* at anything like its face value, we are even less in agreement. Shakespeare's attitude to love was not unusual in Elizabethan poetry, but we must not explain it away, or rather, profess to do so in terms of fashion. Great poetry is not written by fashion. A convention may help to release the poet's inspiration, but it does not make it. Moreover, the great man is often in part the archetype of his age, and to understand Shakespeare is to understand Elizabethan and Jacobean England.

We know nothing positive about Shakespeare's schooling. We cannot even be certain that he went to Stratford Grammar School. There is no reason to believe that his education was in any way remarkable. The only school-masters depicted in the plays are pedants. It seems to have provided him with a tolerable knowledge of Latin, and a more than remarkable command of his mother tongue. As a preparation, it may have been valuable. As a formative influence, it might as well never have existed.

A tradition suggests that Shakespeare worked for a time in his father's business. Whether its failure, marital difficulties, or dramatic ambitions were responsible for his departure from Stratford, we cannot tell. It is probable that the three causes were combined. 'Home-keeping youth haue euer homely wits', and Shakespeare, like other Stratford men, would be unwilling to forgo the prospects of advancement and fortune in London. The decline in his father's prosperity during the years of the poet's adolescence would have determined him to acquire enough money himself to be above financial worry. It is ludicrous to infer from his various lawsuits that he was miserly. The Elizabethan age was an age of litigation, and there is no suggestion that the actions in which he was concerned were frivolous or vexatious. Some biographers seem unaccountably to regret that he received a substantial income from his work.

The scene in *The Two Gentlemen of Verona* in which Valentine embraces the profession of outlaw may be a symbolic representation of Shakespeare's enrolment as an actor in a strolling company, but one cannot tell. It is, at least, a little more credible than the tale of holding horses' heads or the legend of the deer-stealing.

As evidence for the ill-success of the marriage, we may quote Orsino's advice to Cesario :

> Let still the woman take
> An elder then her selfe. so weares she to him ;

35

THE VOYAGE TO ILLYRIA

So swayes she leuell in her husbands heart . . .
For women are as Roses, whose faire flowre
Being once displaid, doth fall that verie howre.

This evidence is accepted even by Sir Sidney Lee. In
the same passage, Shakespeare generously blames himself :

Our fancies are more giddie and vnfirme . . .
Then womens are.

Indeed, its inauspicious start made failure almost inevitable :

By Loue, the yong, and tender wit
Is turn'd to folly, blasting in the Bud,
Loosing his verdure, euen in the prime,
And all the faire effects of future hopes.

Some have supposed that Adriana in *The Comedy of
Errors* is a portrait of Ann, and if the first scene of Act II is
a description of Shakespeare's home-life, his departure is
understandable :

The venome clamors of a iealous woman,
Poisons more deadly then a mad dogges tooth.

However that may be, Shakespeare, soon after the birth
of twins, Judith and Hamnet, in 1585, left Stratford. We
know nothing of the next seven years of his life. He
may have been a schoolmaster in the country before he
found his way to the London stage, as a reliable tradition
states, and this finds some measure of confirmation in a
rather cryptic allusion in Marston's *What You Will*.

36

Others think that he may have been a tutor to the young Earl of Southampton, to whom his mother was distantly related. The Stratford lawsuit about some of his mother's property, which bears some resemblance to the Navarre contention in *Love's Labour's Lost*, was brought to London in 1589, and Shakespeare's name was mentioned in connexion with it. It is possible that he came to London expecting to become a small farmer. With the failure of the lawsuit, he was obliged to look about for a livelihood and so drifted into the theatre. But this must remain conjecture until we have fuller evidence. All we can assert positively is that he carried away from Stratford a love of the Warwickshire countryside which had an enduring influence on his work.

When we turn to the literary influences, our task is less hazardous, and our first clue is the pronouncement of Holofernes in *Love's Labour's Lost* that ' *Ouiddius Naso* was the man '. If Holofernes is a caricature of the Stratford schoolmaster who taught Shakespeare Latin, we may suppose that it was then that the poet acquired a taste for Ovid, especially *The Metamorphoses*, which never left him. It is even possible that when he showed his master his earliest verses, they were criticized thus :

Here are onely numbers ratefied, but for the elegancie, facilitie, and golden cadence of poesie *caret*.

Others have suggested that *Holofernes* is a rough anagram of *Iohn Florio*, who had compiled an English-Italian dictionary, and who was to publish in 1603 a translation of the *Essais* of Montaigne. This is also possible. Shakespeare and Florio had, in the Earl of Southampton, a common patron, and at some stage of their careers, their paths must have crossed.

Some critics have expressed surprise that Shakespeare was more interested in a poet of perceptibly inferior gifts, and that he shows little trace of first-hand acquaintance with Virgil. But this is to misunderstand the contemporary situation. It was an axiom of Elizabethan literary criticism that the modern poet, at best, could only hope to imitate the classics. He could not presume to equal them, and Shakespeare knew what he wanted. If the ancient world was to him mainly *terra incognita*, Ovid's *Metamorphoses* constituted a guide-book, and to the attacks of the University wits, the upstart crow could reply, ' Et ego in Arcadia vixi '. It is clear, from every line of investigation, that Ovid's *Metamorphoses* were to Shakespeare what Lemprière's *Classical Dictionary* and Spence's *Polymetis* were to Keats. Nor must we minimize Ovid's merits. There is a charm in his work which the Renascence, with its love of narrative for its own sake, was quick to perceive. The myths of the ancient world were, too, the case-material of the practitioners of the rudimentary psychology of the time. It is not without interest that the Freudians of the present day have taken over some of the legendary names to typify such well-marked traits and states as narcissism and Oedipus complex.

To Shakespeare, with his deep interest and curiosity concerning human motives, *The Metamorphoses* were a never-ending source of inspiration, and an examination of the legends which influenced his work most, and of the particular passages that he echoed, gives us a further method of approach in our investigation into the working of his mind and the development of his personality.

TUTELAGE

The present generation does not regard Ovid as a philosopher, but in Shakespeare's day the situation was very different. The *Metamorphoses* are set in a cosmogony postulated by the Pythagoreans, and Shakespeare derived from Ovid the cyclic theory of alternate growth and decay in the world. According to this, everything was a repetition of what had gone before. It is best exemplified in *Sonnet* 123 :

NO ! Time, thou shalt not bost that I doe change,
Thy pyramyds buylt vp with newer might
To me are nothing nouell, nothing strange,
They are but dressings of a former sight :
Our dates are breefe, and therefor we admire,
What thou dost foyst vpon vs that is ould,
And rather make them borne to our desire,
Then thinke that we before haue heard them tould :
Thy registers and thee I both defie,
Not wondring at the present, nor the past,
For thy records, and what we see doth lye,
Made more or les by thy continuall hast :
This I doe vow and this shall euer be,
I will be true dispight thy syeth and thee.

It remains to be observed that Shakespeare took a less optimistic view of the wastage than did Ovid, for he seldom looks forward to the subsequent renewal which Nature brings. His only refuge against the future was a personal act of affirmation, evidenced here in the concluding couplet, the joint immortality of constancy and the verse that enshrines it.

Shakespeare's knowledge of the Latin text is proved

by two instances where he adheres to Ovid, and Golding, whose translation he generally used, diverges ; but he seems to have relied increasingly on the translation. Prospero's farewell to his art is the longest continuous passage obviously derived from Golding, and a comparison of Shakespeare's lines with their original will serve to show the measure of his indebtedness :

Ye Ayres and windes : ye Elues of Hilles, of Brookes, of
    Woods alone,
Of standing Lakes, and of the Night approche ye
    euerychone.
Through helpe of whom (the crooked bankes much
    wondring at the thing)
I haue compelled streames to run cleane backward to their
    spring.
By charmes I make the calme Seas rough and make the
    rough Seas plaine,
And couer all the Skie with Cloudes and chase them thence
    againe.
By charmes I raise and lay the windes, and burst the Vipers
    iaw,
And from the bowels of the Earth both stones and trees doe
    draw.
Whole woods and Forestes I remoue : I make the
    Mountaines shake,
And euen the Earth it selfe to grone and fearfully to quake.
I call vp dead men from their graues : and thee, O lightsome
    Moone
I darken oft, though beaten brasse abate thy perill soone.
Our Sorcerie dimmes the Morning faire, and darkes the
    Sun at Noone.

TUTELAGE

The relevant part of Prospero's speech runs thus :

Ye Elues of hils, brooks, standing lakes & groues,
And ye, that on the sands with printlesse foote
Doe chase the ebbing-*Neptune*, and doe flie him
When he comes backe : you demy-Puppets, that
By Moon-shine doe the greene sowre Ringlets make,
Whereof the Ewe not bites : and you, whose pastime
Is to make midnight-Mushrumps, that reioyce
To heare the solemne Curfewe, by whose ayde
(Weake Masters though ye be) I haue bedymn'd
The Noone-tide Sun, call'd forth the mutenous windes,
And twixt the greene Sea, and the azur'd vault
Set roaring warre : To the dread ratling Thunder
Haue I giuen fire, and rifted *Ioues* stowt Oke
With his owne Bolt : The strong bass'd promontorie
Haue I made shake, and by the spurs pluckt vp
The Pyne, and Cedar.   Graues at my command
Haue wak'd their sleepers, op'd, and let 'em forth
By my so potent Art.

In J. M. Robertson's *Montaigne and Shakespeare*, despite
the author's habit of seeing parallels invisible to the unpre-
judiced reader, abundant evidence is put forward to prove
that Shakespeare read Florio's translation of Montaigne's
Essais shortly before *Hamlet* was written.   From the fact
that Montaigne echoes do not appear in the Quarto of
1603, Robertson assumes that they were added afterwards.
The theory is untenable, since the echoes occur in the more
philosophical passages which would naturally be omitted
in the piratical version of the play.   It seems certain that
Shakespeare had read some of the essays in MS., or, since

the book was licensed in 1601 and not published till 1603, he may even have read the proofs. Apart from the very obvious parallel between Gonzalo's description in *The Tempest* of the Golden Age and Montaigne's essay on the cannibals, it is in *Hamlet, Measure for Measure*, and *King Lear* that the influence is most apparent.

After he had read Montaigne, Shakespeare's philosophy owed more to him than to Ovid. This does not impugn his originality. He did not take over Montaigne's thought uncritically, but the fact that his meditations came to be those of Hamlet and the Duke in *Measure for Measure* must be ascribed to the new influence. Much in Hamlet's third and fourth soliloquies and in the Duke's ' Be absolute for death ' speech is clearly derived from Florio's translation. The *Essaies* did not teach Shakespeare how or even what to think, but they coincided with the change in his work, and helped to clarify its expression.

Shakespeare used Holinshed's *Chronicle* for close on ten years as a quarry for historical plays, but there is no evidence that his debt was more than an obvious one. Holinshed valued everyone by the criterion of success. Shakespeare seems to have been more interested in the psychology of failure, apart from the fact that it offered a better subject for a play. It was natural that Shakespeare should identify himself with Henry VI, and still more with Richard II, but the English Histories are more impersonal than the other plays of the same period. They are relevant to this study mainly as exhibiting the stages by which the poet acquired mastery of his craft as a dramatist in the manipulation of his source-material, so that when the time came, he was able to write tragedy, adapting his sources with the assurance born of long practice.

TUTELAGE

Mr. Murry's essay in *Countries of the Mind* II is an admirable exposition of Shakespeare's debt to North's translation of Plutarch's *Lives of the noble Grecians and Romans*. All that need be said here is that Plutarch widened his sympathies and deepened his understanding. Though it is easy to exaggerate questions of influence, it is reasonable to suppose that part of the superiority of *Julius Caesar* and *Antony and Cleopatra* to *Henry IV* and *Henry V* is due to the difference of source-material. North, with all his faults, was a great translator, and Plutarch, with all his, a fascinating biographer.

Mr. Richmond Noble's book, *Shakespeare's Biblical Knowledge*, has demonstrated that the poet's knowledge of the Bible was considerable, and that he used not only the Bishops', but also the Genevan version, and that he was greatly influenced by the Prayer Book Psalter. Moreover, many of the passages concerned do not occur in chapters read in church on Sundays. Mr. Noble shows that the poet was conversant with no less than forty-two books of the Bible, and that he scarcely made a blunder in his use of scriptural passages :

In the earlier plays Scriptural allusions are fairly easy to detect, but as the plays progress, the references become more idiomatic and more closely woven into the text.

After 1597, Shakespeare apparently relied mainly on the Genevan-Tomson version.

There is one type of Biblical echo with which Mr. Noble does not deal. An example was first pointed out by Whiter in 1794, an example of purely verbal borrowing. In *Measure for Measure*, the Duke says :

THE VOYAGE TO ILLYRIA

For if our vertues
Did not goe forth of vs, 'twere all alike
As if we had them not : Spirits are not finely touch'd,
But to fine issues,

and this is derived from Mark v. 25–31 :

And there was a certaine woman, which was diseased
with an issue of blood twelue yeeres. . . .   When shee heard
of Iesus, shee came in the prease behind, and touched his
garment. . . .   And immediatly when Iesus did know in
himselfe the vertue that went out of him, he turned him
. . . about in the prease, and said . . . Who did touch me ?
(*Geneva version.*)

The poet and dramatist to whom Shakespeare owed
most was Marlowe. He referred to his translation of
Hero and Leander twice, quoting from it once, and there
are numerous echoes from it, in the *Sonnets*, in *Love's
Labour's Lost*, in *Richard III*, and in *The Tempest*.
Clarence's dream in *Richard III* contains echoes from the
second Sestiad of Marlowe's poem :

Leander striu'd, the waues about him wound,
And puld him to the bottome, where the ground
Was strewd with pearle, and in low corrall groues
Sweet singing Meremaids, sported with their loues
On heapes of heauie gold, and tooke great pleasure
To spurne in carelesse sort, the shipwracke treasure.

Me thought I sawe a thousand fearfull wracks,
Ten thousand men, that fishes gnawed vpon,

TUTELAGE

Wedges of gold, great anchors, heapes of pearle,
Inestimable stones, vnualued Iewels,
All scattred in the bottome of the Sea,
Some lay in dead mens sculs, and in those holes,
Where eies did once inhabite, there were crept
As twere in scorne of eies reflecting gems.

The probability that the second passage is an echo of the
first is borne out by one of Ariel's songs in *The Tempest* :

Full fadom fiue thy Father lies,
Of his bones are Corrall made :
Those are pearles that were his eies,
Nothing of him that doth fade,
But doth suffer a Sea-change
Into something rich, & strange.
Sea Nimphs hourly ring his knell.
Harke now I heare them, ding-dong bell.

The argument is clinched by the fact that Ariel's other
song :

Come vnto these yellow sands,
    and then take hands :
Curtsied when you haue, and kist
    the wilde waues whist,

is manifestly an echo of another passage from Marlowe's
poem where Hero is describing her tower :

Far from the towne (where all is whist and still,
Saue that the sea playing on yellow sand,
Sends foorth a ratling murmure to the land . . .)
My turret stands.

These echoes of a dead poet contribute something to the supernatural beauty of Ariel's songs. Shakespeare must have read the poem in MS., as the echoes begin before its publication in 1598.

The *New Cambridge* editors have shown that Touchstone's remark :

It strikes a man more dead then a great reckoning in a little roome,

echoes a line from Marlowe's *Jew of Malta*, and refers to Marlowe's death, which occurred in a brawl in the private room of a tavern, and of which the ostensible cause was the reckoning. It is possible, too, that Hamlet's praise of the play that ' was cauiary to the generall ' was intended as a tribute to Marlowe and Nashe's *Tragedy of Dido Queen of Carthage*, which it resembles in style and subject.

Marlowe himself may have learnt from *Henry VI* some lessons about the writing of historical plays, which he found useful in *Edward II*. But it is clear that *Richard II* was an attempt—in Swinburne's opinion, an unsuccessful one—to rival Marlowe's play. Another history, *Richard III*, is so Marlovian in style, that Robertson, prince of disintegrators, pronounced against Shakespeare's authorship.

Marlowe's conception of tragedy was a considerable advance on that of his predecessors. In place of the medieval idea :

Tragedie is to seyn a certeyn storie . . .
Of him that stood in greet prosperitee
And is yfallen out of heigh degree
Into miserie, and endeth wrecchedly,

46

TUTELAGE

Marlowe substituted a tragic hero who was brought to his doom by the excess of some quality. Tamburlaine is ruined by his lust for power, Faustus by his lust for knowledge, Barabas by his lust for gold, Edward II by his excessive love for favourites. This is not far from the Shakespearean conception expressed through the mouth of Hamlet :

> So oft it chaunces in particuler men,
> That for some vicious mole of nature in them . . .
> By their ore-growth of some complexion
> Oft breaking downe the pales and forts of reason,
> Or by some habit, that too much ore-leauens
> The forme of plausiue manners, that these men
> Carrying I say the stamp of one defect
> Being Natures liuery, or Fortunes starre,
> His vertues els be they as pure as grace,
> As infinite as man may vndergoe,
> Shall in the generall censure take corruption
> From that particuler fault : the dram of euill
> Doth all the noble substance antidote
> To his owne scandle.

Shakespeare may also have learnt from Marlowe to portray a hero magnified so as to dwarf the other characters of the play, an essential characteristic of most Shakespearean tragedy.

There was, also, a deeper debt than any yet mentioned. Marlowe bequeathed to his successor the greatest legacy poet ever received, the blank verse line. But this is become such a commonplace of literary history that we do not propose to enlarge on it.

THE VOYAGE TO ILLYRIA

It is often said that Shakespeare learned from Greene the portrayal of female character. But the only heroines who bear much resemblance to Greene's are those of the Romances, Imogen and Hermione. The former may be explained as due rather to a similarity of plot, while *The Winter's Tale* is a dramatization of Greene's novel *Pandosto*. In any event, nearly twenty years separate this portion of their work, and the portrayer of Beatrice, Rosalind, Cordelia and Cleopatra had little to learn from Greene. In defiance of academic opinion, it must be said that Greene's heroines are both wooden and priggish, and their admired virtues are a result of the story in which they find themselves. They are merely patient Griseldas, and never come to life. If Shakespeare owed anything to Greene, it was a knowledge of the just use of prose and verse in a play, and that subtle balance between seriousness and comedy which is a noteworthy feature of so many of Shakespeare's plays.

A far more real influence was the dramatic work of Lyly. It is not too much to say that every characteristic of Shakespearean comedy, except the skilful blending of prose and verse, is to be found in Lyly. Farcical scenes like those between the Dromios, between Moth, Armado and Costard, between Launce and Speed, and between Launcelot and old Gobbo ; wit contests between persons of rank, Boyet and the French ladies, Portia and Nerissa, Beatrice and Benedick, the use of parallel plots, the use of song, the pastoral spirit of *As You Like It* and *The Winter's Tale*, the introduction of fairies, and the disguising of girls as boys, these are a few of the dramatic devices which Shakespeare learned from Lyly. But his indebtedness is more profound, though less tangible, in the creation of atmosphere.

TUTELAGE

The world of Shakespearean comedy is fundamentally the same as Lyly's. The conventions, the style, the very air we breathe is the same. There can be no doubt that Shakespeare's comedies would have been very different had not Lyly preceded him.

Not only was Shakespeare generally indebted to his forerunner, but more than fifty specific borrowings have been pointed out, and these include such famous passages as 'O limed soule, that struggling to be free, Art more ingaged', 'I am a great eater of beefe, and I beleeue that does harme to my wit', the precepts of Polonius, and the criticisms of the male sex made by Beatrice.

Furthermore, Shakespeare learned from Lyly how to write prose, and though in 1 *Henry IV* he poked fun at the excesses of Euphuism, he remained to the end of his career profoundly affected by it. In the prose of the earliest comedies, there are few marks of the Lylian style in the actual rhythms and constructions, but, between 1596 and 1600, Shakespeare fell under the spell of *Euphues*. The civilized prose of the great comedies owes much in its constructions, its rhythms, its balance, and its poise to the example of Lyly. It sharpened the edge of his wit, and gave his dialogue more bite and sparkle. Touchstone, Falstaff and Beatrice use a modified form of the style in which its inherent artificiality is toned down. At the end of the century, Shakespeare tired of this, and he began to poke fun at it. In *Hamlet*, it is Osric and Rosencrantz and Guildenstern who speak in the Euphuistic style, and Hamlet parodies it. In the last plays, notably in *The Winter's Tale* and *Cymbeline*, 'where information on matters of fact had to be given to the audience, or where it was desirable to strike a specially ceremonial note', Lyly's influence again made itself felt.

The other University wits are less important. Kyd seems to have written the original Hamlet play, and he neglected few opportunities of putting a ghost on the stage. Peele may have contributed something to Shakespeare's lyrical and pastoral note. But what matters more than an occasional piece of evidence for direct and specific borrowing is the fact that in the decade immediately preceding Shakespeare's début as a dramatist, English drama made an enormous stride forward. When Shakespeare began his career, the drama was already flourishing, and he was not under the necessity of creating an art-form for his genius. It lay ready to his hand. If he had been born twenty years earlier, he might never have written a play.

Before we turn to the plays, however, we must study the two poems that accompanied his dramatic nonage. *Venus and Adonis* and *Lucrece* possessed a popularity in his lifetime that did not altogether depend on their poetic merits.

'The younger sort,' wrote Gabriel Harvey, 'takes much delight in Shakespeare's Venus, & Adonis: but his Lucrece, & his tragedie of Hamlet, Prince of Denmarke, haue it in them, to please the wiser sort.'

Gullio, the sentimental young lover in the second of the Parnassus plays, wishes to have sweet Mr. Shakespeare's picture in his study, and raves about *Venus and Adonis* :

Let this duncified worlde esteeme of Spencer and Chaucer, Ile worshipp sweet Mr. Shakspeare, and to

TUTELAGE

honoure him will lay his Venus, and Adonis vnder my
pillowe, as wee reade of one (I do not well remember
his name) but I am sure he was a kinge, slept with Homer
vnder his beds heade.

Thomas Freeman, writing in 1614, addressed Shakespeare
in a sonnet which indicates one reason for the continued
popularity of the poem :

Vertues or vices theame to thee all one is :
Who loues chaste life, there's *Lucrece* for a Teacher :
Who list read lust there's *Venus* and *Adonis*,
True modell of a most lasciuious leatcher.

It was, in fact, the daring sensuality of the poem that
sent it through ten editions in as many years.

It was written in 1592, a year when the plague led
to the closing of the theatres, and it was printed by Richard
Field, a fellow townsman of Shakespeare. We have
already discussed its dedication to the Earl of Southampton.
The exhortations of Venus to Adonis are so similar to the
themes of the first group of sonnets, in which Shakespeare
urges his patron to marry, that it seems certain that they
were written at the same time. Southampton was bound
to recognize the similarity of theme, though it is by no
means necessary to assume that the poet was writing at
the request of relatives who wished to see the Earl married.
In this connexion, lines 127–132, 163–174, 751–768, and
1075–1080 are noteworthy.

The general spirit of the poem is not unlike that of
Hero and Leander. *Venus and Adonis* is not so clear-cut
and brilliant as Marlowe's masterpiece, but the decoration

is more leisurely, more sensuous, and drawn more directly from life. Its fault, if one can call it so, is a youthful excess of rhetoric, which is most apparent in the frequent antithesis and epigram. The poem is nevertheless masterly, and it contains none of the weakness to be expected in a first volume of verse. Shakespeare, though he calls it ' the first heir ' of his invention, was already a practised poet. He had exercised his pen in the drama, and it is in his early plays that we must seek the hand of the prentice.

The main source of *Venus and Adonis* was his favourite Ovid, and the stories of Adonis and of Hermaphroditus in the *Metamorphoses* provide the bulk of his material. Meres was justly praising when he said :

> so the sweete wittie soule of *Ouid* liues in mellifluous & hony-tongued *Shakespeare*, witnes his *Venus* and *Adonis*, his *Lucrece* . . .

Shakespeare recaptures the spirit of Ovid to perfection, though he is far more outspoken in his descriptions, and he is writing much more than a mere imitation. Apart from the likely echoes of Ann's wooing of William ten years before, the poem is filled with the influence of the Warwickshire countryside. There is more description of Nature than in any other work of Shakespeare, and it contains a precise, almost Wordsworthian, observation of flowers and animal life, in which he seldom afterwards indulged. We have a glimpse of

> a diuedapper peering through a waue,
> Who being lookt on, ducks as quickly in,

and of the milch-doe,

TUTELAGE

whose swelling dugs do ake,
Hasting to feed her fawne, hid in some brake.

There is a long and vivid description of the stallion, a delicate passage about the timid flying hare, and the famous lines which so delighted Keats :

The snaile, whose tender hornes being hit,
Shrinks backward in his shellie caue with paine,
And, there all smoothred vp, in shade doth sit,
Long after fearing to creepe forth againe.

There are, too, innumerable references to birds, beasts, flowers and plants. Nearly all the imagery is drawn from Nature, though there is a mention of a shrill tapster, of the deadly bullet, and of a traveller, whose lantern is extinguished in the middle of a dark wood. We hear of the washing being spread over the rose-bushes, of an earthquake, of an adder blocking the path, of the sluice-gates on the river, of fairies tripping on the green, and nymphs with long dishevelled hair dancing on the sands. There are references to birds in the snare of the fowler, to the lark mounting in the sky from his moist cabinet, to crows and falcons, to the mellow plum dropping from the tree, to mulberries, cherries and caterpillars. We can see that Shakespeare had a taste for painting, and that he considered that art should not imitate, but surpass life. All these details, and many more, can be gathered from the imagery of the poem.

There are lines of exquisite beauty :

Leading him prisoner in a red rose chaine . . .

THE VOYAGE TO ILLYRIA

> Looke how a bright star shooteth from the skye ;
> So glides he in the night from Venus eye,

and, best of all, this stanza with its drowsy, sensuous, haunting cadences :

> Hot, faint, and wearie, with her hard imbracing,
> Like a wild bird being tam'd with too much handling,
> Or as the fleet-foot Roe that's tyr'd with chasing,
> Or like the froward infant stild with dandling :
>   He now obayes, and now no more resisteth,
>   VVhile she takes all she can, not all she listeth.

There are occasional lines of a deeper power :

> And bid suspition double locke the dore . . .
> Call it not loue, for loue to heauen is fled,
> Since sweating lust on earth vsurpt his name.

Sometimes the poet is led into a not wholly successful conceit :

> A lillie prisond in a gaile of snow,

but, at other times, he is brilliantly epigrammatic without ceasing to be poetic :

> She's loue ; she loues, and yet she is not lou'd.

He often obtains a hard, brilliant effect unlike romantic narrative poetry by sudden touches of realism that verge on occasion towards caricature. Against the mythological background, he places figures that have been observed with a detached and almost satiric eye :

> He wrings her nose, he strikes her on the cheekes,
> He bends her fingers, holds her pulses hard,
> He chafes her lips, a thousand wayes he seekes,
> To mend the hurt, that his vnkindnesse mard.

> The loue-sicke Queene began to sweate.

> Forst to consent, but neuer to obey,
> Panting he lies, and breatheth in her face.

Sometimes there is an ironic hyperbole, as when Venus is made to say of Adonis's lips :

> Oh neuer let their crimson liueries weare,
> And as they last, their verdour still endure,
> To driue infection from the dangerous yeare :
>   That the star-gazers hauing writ on death,
>   May say, the plague is banisht by thy breath.

In such passages as these we are in the same atmosphere as *Love's Labour's Lost*, with its mockery of the exaggerations of love.

In one or two passages Shakespeare comes down rather heavily on the side of the angels, as in the moralizing about love and lust ; and from Venus's prophecy at the end, one is led to suppose that Shakespeare had already entered the bondage of the Dark Lady. Instead of the frank, and almost gay, sensuality of the first half of the poem, in which we feel that the poet supports the goddess in her

E   55

designs on Adonis, we have a grim account of the realities of love :

It shall be fickle, false, and full of fraud,
Bud, and be blasted, in a breathing while,
The bottome poyson, and the top ore-strawd
VVith sweets, that shall the truest sight beguile,
The strongest bodie shall it make most weake,
Strike the wise dumbe, & teach the foole to speake . . .

It shall suspect where is no cause of feare,
It shall not feare where it should most mistrust,
It shall be mercifull, and too seueare,
And most deceiuing, when it seemes most iust . . .

It shall be cause of warre, and dire euents,
And set dissention twixt the sonne, and sire,
Subiect, and seruill to all discontents :
As drie combustious matter is to fire.

There are passages that look forward to the plays, or echo the early sonnets. Adonis's distinction between love and lust is frequently made by the poet :

Loue comforteth like sun-shine after raine,
But lusts effect is tempest after sunne,
Loues gentle spring doth alwayes fresh remaine,
Lusts winter comes, ere sommer halfe be donne :
    Loue surfets not, lust like a glutton dies :
    Loue is all truth, lust full of forged lies.

Venus chiding Death looks forward to *Lucrece* :

TUTELAGE

Hard fauourd tyrant, ougly, meagre, leane,
Hatefull diuorce of loue. . . .
Grim-grinning ghost, earths-worme what dost thou meane?
To stifle beautie, and to steale his breath ?

and this passage forms a natural link with the ' grauer
labour' of *Lucrece*, which was published in the following
year.

For his material, Shakespeare again went to Ovid, this
time to the *Fasti* where the story is briefly told, and he
supplemented this with further hints from Chaucer's
Legend of Good Women, from Livy's *History*, from Painter's
Palace of Pleasure, and Daniel's *Complaint of Rosamond*.
Though its subject did not permit of the sensuous decoration
of its predecessor, and some parts of it are a little laboured,
Lucrece exhibits, in its finest passages, a deeper power and
a greater sense of drama.

The imagery is totally different, and the difference
cannot be altogether explained by the changed subject.
One might suppose, as the scene of the poem is mostly
indoors, and at night, that there would be less imagery
drawn from Nature, and that, owing to the brutal theme
of the story, there would be a grimmer kind of imagery,
but the poet exhibits no acquaintance with Nature, and
nearly all his metaphors are drawn from his reading and
the intercourse of civilized life. Treasure, jewels, gorgeous
fabrics, painted cloths, servitors, sieges and battles, heraldry,
the subtle-shining secrecies writ in the glassy margents of
books, banners, fortresses, pillaging, torches, cities, the
eye of the cockatrice, nocturnal cats, tempestuous seas,
exiled kings, vomiting, poison, rebellion, bankrupts,
beggars, bawds, pawning, trafficking, furnaces, page-boys,

weeping widows, pack-horses, Fortune's wheel, the unicorn, lackeys, grooms, executioners, volcanoes, worms, these are some of the things suggested by the images.

Jewel imagery, based on the idea that chastity is a treasure, is a favourite one with Shakespeare, particularly in *Pericles*. Imagery drawn from tempest and sudden death is the natural accompaniment of a tragic theme in all his work, and *Lucrece* is no exception. The atmosphere is largely obtained by such means. Heraldic imagery and that connected with page-boys, servitors, rich fabrics and paintings came naturally to a middle-class provincial newly introduced to the splendours of a nobleman's town mansion. But there remains the feeling that a good deal of the imagery was laboured, and that it lacks the delicate spontaneity of the earlier poem. It is not so perfectly assimilated as the natural background of *Venus and Adonis*.

What imagery in *Lucrece* is drawn from Nature would seem to be second-hand and the fruit of reading :

> This pale Swan in her watrie nest,
> Begins the sad Dirge of her certaine ending.

> Come Philomele that sing'st of rauishment,
> Make thy sad groue in my disheueld heare.

> Here with a Cockeatrice dead killing eye,
> He rowseth vp himselfe, and makes a pause.

In *Lucrece*, we observe Shakespeare's use of birds and beasts as symbols, a device he employed in *The Phoenix and the Turtle* and in the great tragedies :

TUTELAGE

No noise but Owles, & wolues death-boding cries.
The wolfe hath ceazd his pray, the poor lamb cries.
Todes infect faire founts with venome mud.
The Crow may bath his coaleblacke wings in mire.

Several themes which recur in the plays are first found
here. Tarquin's threat to murder the groom in order
to cast suspicion on him reappears in *Macbeth*, and the
imagery shows a most astonishing resemblance. The
description of Lucrece in bed is a forerunner of the similar
scene in *Cymbeline* :

> VVithout the bed her other faire hand was,
> On the greene couerlet whose perfect white
> Showed like an Aprill dazie on the grasse,
> VVith pearlie swet resembling dew of night,

and the long description of the painting of the siege of
Troy not only looks forward to *Troilus and Cressida* and to
the Hecuba speeches in *Hamlet*, but would seem to be
derived from an actual painting, which, perhaps, hung in
Southampton's house :

> In AIAX and VLYSSES, ô what Art
> Of Phisiognomy might one behold !
> The face of eyther cypher'd eythers heart,
> Their face, their manners most expreslie told,
> In AIAX eyes blunt rage and rigour rold,
>   But the mild glance that slie VLYSSES lent,
>   Shewed deepe regard and smiling gouernment . . .

> Here one mans hand leand on anothers head,
> His nose being shadowed by his neighbours eare,

Here one being throng'd, bears back all boln, & red,
Another smotherd, seemes to pelt and sweare,
And in their rage such signes of rage they beare,
  As but for losse of NESTORS golden words,
  It seem'd they would debate with angrie swords.

Shakespeare evidently had a keen appreciation of painting, and this is brought out in the lines on Hecuba :

In her the Painter had anathomiz'd
Times ruine, beauties wracke, and grim cares raign,
Her cheeks with chops and wrincles were disguiz'd,
Of what shee was, no semblance did remaine :
Her blew bloud chang'd to blacke in euerie vaine,
  VVanting the spring, that those shrunke pipes had fed.

The picture of Troy appears, years later, in *Cymbeline*, where the similarity of situation might send the poet's mind back to the poem.

Coleridge said that in *Lucrece* Shakespeare ' gave ample proof of his possession of a most profound, energetic, and philosophical mind '. The evidence for this is mostly contained in the protracted soliloquy of over two hundred and fifty lines, in which Lucrece rails at Opportunity. It is a foretaste of the tirades of the early Histories, and looks forward to the soliloquies of the maturer plays. It is extremely artificial, but it is magnificent rhetoric, exemplifying its author's amazing facility of expression and his daring virtuosity. At times, it rises to poetry of considerable power :

Misshapen time, copesmate of vgly night,
Swift subtle post, carrier of grieslie care,

TUTELAGE

Eater of youth, false slaue to false delight :
Base watch of woes, sins packhorse, vertues snare,
Thou noursest all, and murthrest all that are . . .
Times glorie is to calme contending Kings,
To vnmaske falshood, and bring truth to light,
To stampe the seale of time in aged things,
To wake the morne, and Centinell the night,
To wrong the wronger till he render right,
    To ruinate proud buildings with thy howres,
    And smeare with dust their glitring golden towrs . . .

Thou ceaselesse lackie to Eternitie.

This last line is worthy of Shakespeare at his greatest.
Railing on Time and Death is a favourite pursuit of
characters in the early plays, and in this, also, *Lucrece* is
the seed of much of Shakespeare's development. He
never again essayed to write a long narrative poem. It
is most unlikely that he ever again had the leisure till the
last years of his life, when he would be unwilling to forgo
the advantages of the dramatic form. Even *Lucrece*, from
the strictly narrative point of view, contains too much
direct speech and too little action.

A Lover's Complaint raises several problems that we
are not in a position to solve. Either it was written
before the other two poems, or it was composed at a time
when Shakespeare was not exerting his full powers. It
is quite isolated from the rest of his work.

In the last chapter, it was claimed that the *Sonnets* were
of vital importance for a proper understanding of the
poet's development, and we have already seen how his
two long poems reflect his personal thought. We now

propose to show how, despite Sir Sidney Lee's point-blank assertion to the contrary, the drama of the *Sonnets* had its repercussions in the early plays.

Love's Labour's Lost, one of the earliest plays, was almost certainly written for Southampton. He revived it for James the First's queen, and the obviously personal hits would be unintelligible to the audience of the ordinary playhouse. It is not part of our present purpose to identify all the topical allusions and personal satire in the play, but it cannot be doubted that Chapman is represented by Boyet, and that he, therefore, is the rival poet of the *Sonnets*. On Boyet's first entrance, the Princess addresses him thus :

> Good Lord *Boyet*, my beautie though but meane,
> Needes not the painted florish of your prayse :
> Beautie is bought by iudgement of the eye,
> Not vttred by base sale of chapmens tongues.

The point is further developed by Biron, who may represent, and may even have been played by, Shakespeare himself :

> This fellow peckes vp Wit as Pidgions Pease,
> And vtters it againe when God dooth please.
> He is Witts Pedler, and retales his wares :
> At Wakes and Wassels, meetings, markets, Faires,
> And we that sell by grosse, the Lord doth know,
> Haue not the grace to grace it with such show . . .
> This is the floure that smyles on euery one,
> To shew his teeth as white as Whalës bone,
> And consciences that will not die in debt,
> Pay him the due of honie-tonged *Boyet*.

TUTELAGE

This speech has many affinities with the group of sonnets in which Shakespeare complains of a rival :

> I Neuer saw that you did painting need,
> And therefore to your faire no painting set,
> I found (or thought I found) you did exceed,
> The barren tender of a Poets debt.
>
> My toung-tide Muse in manners holds her still,
> While comments of your praise richly compil'd,
> Reserue their Character with goulden quill,
> And precious phrase by all the Muses fil'd.
>
> So is it not with me as with that Muse,
> Stird by a painted beauty to his verse,
> Who heauen it selfe for ornament doth vse,
> And euery faire with his faire doth reherse. . . .
>   Let them say more that like of heare-say well,
>   I will not prayse that purpose not to sell.
>
>   When they haue deuisde,
> What strained touches Rhethorick can lend,
> Thou truly faire, wert truly simpathizde,
> In true plaine words, by thy true telling friend.
>
> Who is it that sayes most, which can say more,
> Then this rich praise, that you alone, are you ?

The theme of *Love's Labour's Lost* is the overthrowing of honour by the advent of women. The King and his three courtiers break their solemn vows almost without a struggle. Don Armado, though he clings to his vocab-

ulary as to a life-belt, is swept away by his passion for
Jaquenetta. The story is double-edged. It satirizes those
who endeavour to live a cloistered existence, but it also
reflects, though gaily, the first impact of the Dark Lady on
the friendship of the *Sonnets*. Berowne confesses that
Rosaline is

> A whitly wanton, with a veluet brow,
> With two pitch balles stucke in her face for eyes,
> I, and by heauen, one that will do the deede,
> Though *Argus* were her eunuch and her garde,

but to the King he justifies his love :

> Is Ebonie like her ?   O word deuine !
> A wife of such wood were felicitie . . .
> No face is fayre that is not full so blacke.

The King declares that black is the badge of Hell, and
Berowne replies that Rosaline is

>   borne to make blacke fayre.
> Her fauour turnes the fashion of the dayes,
> For natiue blood is counted paynting now.

The inference is that Shakespeare was confessing his
enslavement to the Dark Lady, though we hear no mention
yet of the second stage in the story, the enslavement
of his friend, and the poet's surrender.   For this, we must
look farther ahead. *The Two Gentlemen of Verona* is
similar in atmosphere to the *Sonnets* and to *Love's Labour's
Lost*. It, also, describes how passion makes men forget

the duties of friendship. Montemayor's story, the only discoverable source, is complicated by the introduction of Valentine, and with it, the conflict between love and friendship which is resolved by Valentine's surrender of Silvia to his friend Proteus.

Shakespeare has identified himself most with Valentine, the wronged friend, whose description of Proteus bears a most striking resemblance to the portrait of the youth of the *Sonnets* :

> And though my selfe haue beene an idle Trewant,
> Omitting the sweet benefit of time
> To cloath mine age with Angel-like perfection :
> Yet hath Sir *Protheus* . . .
> Made vse, and faire aduantage of his daies . . .
> And in a word (for far behinde his worth
> Comes all the praises that I now bestow.)
> He is compleat in feature, and in minde.

The Duke replies :

> He is as worthy for an Empresse loue,
> As meet to be an Emperors Councellor.

The dénouement of the play, when Valentine forgives Proteus, is a dramatization of *Sonnet* 40, which we have already quoted :

> I doe forgiue thy robb'rie gentle theefe
> Although thou steale thee all my pouerty :
> And yet loue knowes it is a greater griefe
> To beare loues wrong, then hates knowne iniury.

THE VOYAGE TO ILLYRIA

These are Valentine's words :

> And once againe, I doe receiue thee honest ;
> Who by Repentance is not satisfied,
> Is nor of heauen, nor earth ; for these are pleas'd :
> By Penitence th'Eternalls wrath's appeas'd :
> And that my loue may appeare plaine and free,
> All that was mine, in *Siluia*, I giue thee.

His relinquishment of Silvia is more quixotic than Platonic, as the play stands, and the most natural explanation would seem to be that Shakespeare was too close to a similar event in his own life to master its implications, and make the dramatic motives clear. Reconciliation, in his early plays, was always the acid test under which his invention failed, notably in *Much Ado About Nothing* and *As You Like It*, and these two causes, rather than any theory of revision, must be taken as the explanation of the feeble splutter in which the play expires.

The advice of Proteus to Sir Thurio, though quoted by Sir Sidney Lee as a proof that the *Sonnets* were insincere, considered dispassionately, proves the direct opposite :

> You must lay Lime, to tangle her desires
> By walefull Sonnets, whose composed Rimes
> Should be full fraught with seruiceable vowes.

If Shakespeare's had been insincere, if they had been full fraught with serviceable vows, if he had praised his patron for what he could get out of him, it is clear that he would never have had the brazen effrontery to write this passage.

TUTELAGE

There is one speech in the play which is particularly interesting, the soliloquy of Proteus in Act II, scene vi :

Loue bad mee sweare, and Loue bids me for-sweare . . .
At first I did adore a twinkling Starre,
But now I worship a celestiall Sunne :
Vn-heedfull vowes may heedfully be broken . . .
And *Siluia* (witnesse heauen that made her faire)
Shewes *Iulia* but a swarthy Ethiope.

This is but one of many indications in the early work that Shakespeare sought in those he loved a reflection of himself. Inevitably he was disappointed. The myriad-minded could find only a fragment of his personality in each of his lovers. Ann, Southampton, the Dark Lady, all failed to satisfy his whole nature. At first, the friend seemed to offer a marriage of true minds, as *Sonnet* 31 shows :

Thou art the graue where buried loue doth liue,
Hung with the trophies of my louers gone,
Who all their parts of me to thee did giue,
That due of many, now is thine alone.
    Their images I lou'd, I view in thee,
    And thou (all they) hast all the all of me.

But, however much he sublimated the desires of the flesh, he was too human to find a complete solution in this relationship. Those who regret his passion for the Dark Lady forget that his greatness sprang from his humanity. Dante became a great poet by his renunciation, Shakespeare by his acceptance of life. Dante is honoured : Shakespeare loved.

The imagery of *Love's Labour's Lost* and of *The Two Gentlemen of Verona* is not very revealing. Indeed, there is astonishingly little of it. Shakespeare gets most of his effects by direct statements ; his metaphors and similes seem, at this time, to have been only decoration. In the later plays, meaning and metaphor are one. In this respect, the poems are more mature than the plays written at the same time. They were written with greater care. Shakespeare was free of the fetters of dramatic form, and he was not under the necessity of making them understood at a first hearing.

Cormorant devouring time, the favourite theme of the *Sonnets*, reappears in *Love's Labour's Lost*. We have imagery drawn from war and weapons, from books and clocks and clothes, from jewels and coaches, from schools, pickpockets and plays. Nature plays a much smaller part in the imagery than has generally been supposed. Critics seem to have derived their impression of the atmosphere from the two songs at the end, which are a vivid and realistic description of country life. With this exception, the imagery relates to the more obvious changes of the seasons, sneaping frost, snow in May, and hawthorn blossom shaking in the breeze, sun, moon, and dew, the unsullied lily, and the sea.

Shakespeare seems to have been much interested, when he wrote the play, in problems touching on his craft as a writer, in the question of inspiration in poetry, in the use of rhetoric, in the use of language, in orthography, in oddities and innovations of vocabulary, and in the excesses of the aureate style :

TUTELAGE

Taffata phrases, silken tearmes precise,
Three-pilde Hiperboles, spruce affectation :
Figures pedanticall, these sommer flies,
Haue blowne me full of maggot ostentation.

In *The Two Gentlemen of Verona* we find even less
imagery, but more numerous references to classical
mythology, drawn fairly evidently from Ovid. Jewels
occur again, a house falling into decay because it has no
tenant, a snowman melting in the sun, which comes
again in *Richard II*, and the image of the stream which has
been dammed, always a favourite of Shakespeare's, call
for mention. The most interesting images are two which
refer to fawning spaniels, and which were suggested,
perhaps, by Launce's dog, but they are not associated
with sweets and flatterers, as they were to be later in
Shakespeare's work.

The Comedy of Errors is most likely an adaptation of
another man's work, but the reworking has been complete.
Nevertheless, the primitive doggerel in which the Dromios
often speak must belong to a different stratum from the
best scenes. The long speech of Ægeon which opens
the plot is a remarkable piece of condensed narrative,
and sets the involved story firmly on its path, and Adriana's
appeal to her supposed husband in Act II, scene ii, shows
a great advance on the alternately rhymed lines of Act
III, scene ii, but there is much that is contaminated by
doggerel, and obscenity unredeemed by wit.

There is scarcely any imagery in the play. The most
striking is Ægeon's

Though now this grained face of mine be hid
In sap-consuming Winters drizled snow.

69

But this is all that we are entitled to expect in a farce which has little connexion with the rest of Shakespeare's work. It is a good acting play with plenty of life and vigour, and the construction leaves little for criticism.

Romeo and Juliet and *A Midsummer Night's Dream* are the first two plays to exhibit Shakespeare's real power, and, unlike those we have so far discussed, they have retained their popularity to this day. *Romeo and Juliet* is the first play in which imagery played an integral part, both in the creation of atmosphere, and in the light it throws on the main theme, providing what Miss Caroline Spurgeon calls 'undersong'. She has pointed out the prevalence of one group of images relating to light and darkness. ' Each of the lovers thinks of the other as light.' Juliet hangs upon the cheek of night, like a rich jewel in an Ethiope's ear. Her window is the east, and she herself is the sun. Her eyes are stars, the brightness of her cheek would shame the stars as daylight doth a lamp, and even when she is dead, her tomb is a lantern, a feasting presence full of light. Romeo is day in night, he lies upon the wings of night whiter than new snow on a raven's back, and when he dies he will be cut up into a constellation of stars. The lovers can see each other in the darkness. Their love is sudden as the lightning, as violent as an explosion of gunpowder. Romeo's wit is set afire by his own ignorance, like powder in a skilless soldier's flask, the name of Romeo makes Juliet fall down as if shot, and Romeo asks for a potion that will kill him as swiftly as the firing of a cannon.

As Miss Spurgeon says :

The beauty and ardour of young love is seen by Shakespeare as the irradiating glory of sunlight and starlight in a dark world.

Many of the scenes take place at night, and the atmosphere is painted by frequent references to the moon and the stars, to lamps and torches. The background is astonishingly conveyed by references to a grove of sycamores, to a pomegranate tree, to fruit-trees tipped with silver, to the nightingale singing passionately in the warm darkness. There is abundant imagery drawn from Nature. Jocund day stands tiptoe on the misty mountain-tops, well-apparelled April treads on the heels of limping winter, Juliet is light as gossamer, and the wind woos the frozen bosom of the North. This last is a fine example of the way in which Shakespeare preserves the atmosphere of love—even when he is talking of other things. He conceived the love between Romeo and Juliet to be as spontaneous as a flower, a bud which would be ripened by the summer. Romeo's love for Rosaline, on the other hand, is as the bud bit by the envious worm. To Shakespeare, unreturned and hidden love was always that. Concealment, like a worm i'th'bud, feeds on the damask cheek. Perhaps the finest of the nature-images describes Juliet's supposed death :

> Death lies on her like an vntimely frost,
> Vpon the sweetest flower of all the field.

A large proportion of the remaining images relate to religion. Rosaline will not ope her lap to saint-seducing gold. Romeo declares that his eyes will be transparent heretics if ever they look on another woman. Juliet's

hand is a shrine, Romeo a pilgrim. Juliet is a saint to
whom Romeo prays; he offers to be new-baptized for
her, he compares her to a winged messenger of heaven,
and the Friar says that her foot is so light that she will
never wear out the everlasting flint. Love gives Romeo
wings, so that he himself becomes Love. After he has
killed Tybalt, Juliet describes him as a damned saint, the
serpent in Eden, the spirit of the fiend in the mortal paradise
of his sweet flesh. Romeo banished compares himself
to the damned in Hell, because Juliet is his Heaven. The
reason for this set of images can only be that Shakespeare's
religion when he wrote the play was love.

Closely connected with this is a group of images
relating to voyages. Romeo, just before his meeting with
Juliet, says:

> But he that hath the stirrage of my course,
> Direct my sute.

Love is Romeo's pilot, not God, as most editions imply.

> ' Wert thou as farre,' he says,
> ' As that vast shore washt with the farthest sea,
> I should aduenture for such marchandise.'

In his last speech, his death is shipwreck in a tempestuous
sea, but it is clear that he expects to reach the paradise,
the enchanted island of his lover's arms:

> Thou desperate Pilot, now at once run on
> The dashing Rockes, thy seasick weary barke:
> Heeres to my Loue.

TUTELAGE

It seems likely that the idea of passing through a tempest to reach the paradise of love was derived from *Hero and Leander*, in which Leander swims the stormy Hellespont to reach the arms of Hero, though Shakespeare expands the concept by the frequent image of the ship bearing the lover. Death and Love were intimately connected in his mind, and this is clearly shown in the imagery of *Romeo and Juliet*.

Juliet declares that if Romeo is married, the grave is like to be her wedding-bed. 'Old desire doth in his deathbed lie, And young affection gapes to be his heire.' Affliction is enamoured of Romeo, and he is wedded to calamity. When he climbs down from the balcony, Juliet sees him as dead in the bottom of the tomb. Juliet, supposed dead, is deflowered by death. Death is a monster gorged with the dearest morsel of the earth. Unsubstantial death is amorous, and he has sucked the honey of her breath. Worms are Juliet's paramours, and her vault is like a brilliantly illuminated wedding-feast. When Romeo is told of her death, he cries, 'Iuliet, I will lie with thee to night.' Death is love-devouring, and the churchyard is hungry. Romeo dreams that his lady came and found him dead, and breathed such life with kisses in his lips, that he revived and was an emperor. The whole play is shot through with this imagery, and there can be no doubt that it throws a great deal of light on Shakespeare's own conception of the play, especially with regard to the person responsible for the tragedy.

Critics who fail to look below the surface assume that the Friar expresses Shakespeare's own view of the tragedy, but Friar Lawrence, who would seem to be intended as a commentator, is, frankly, a bore. His warning against passion, 'These violent delights haue violent ends,' has led Mr. Masefield, in an unfortunate moment, to declare that love

makes the sweet-natured girl a deceitful scheming liar . . . The only apparent good of the disease is that it destroys its victim swiftly.

In actual fact, the meddling Friar, anxious to save his face, is quite as much responsible for the tragedy as are the passion-driven lovers. If he had advised Juliet to confess her marriage, the tragedy would not have occurred. The tradition which associates the poet with the witty, bawdy, imaginative Mercutio has much more to recommend it, but, from what we have already said, it should be apparent that Shakespeare identified himself, most of all, with Romeo.

One more thing can be inferred from the imagery. There is another group of images relating to war. All through the play, there runs the double theme of love and hate, war and peace. The feud between the Montagues and the Capulets is healed by the death of the lovers. Love conquers hate, as it conquers death :

> Thou art not conquerd, bewties ensigne yet
> Is crymson in thy lips and in thy cheeks,
> And deaths pale flag is not aduanced there.

Romeo and Juliet are sacrifices—atonement for the hatred dividing the families of Verona.

The tragedy is not like any other of Shakespeare's. It

is Fate rather than the tragic flaw which brings about the lovers' doom. Heaven practises stratagems against Juliet. She prays in vain to Pity sitting in the clouds. Romeo defies the stars, and, in the end, he shakes the yoke of inauspicious stars from his world-wearied flesh. But for Fate, the story might have ended differently. Shakespeare's other tragic heroes carry in them the seed of their own destruction. Except for *Antony and Cleopatra*, it is the only tragedy in which the heroine is of equal importance with the hero.

There are many parallels between *Romeo and Juliet* and the *Sonnets*. Some of these are set out by Sir Sidney Lee in his introduction to the facsimile edition of the *Sonnets* (1905), pp. 22–24. One of the most striking is the image of the sun as an object of worship :

> Loe in the Orient when the gracious light,
> Lifts vp his burning head, each vnder eye
> Doth homage to his new appearing sight,
> Seruing with lookes his sacred maiesty.

This appears in *Romeo and Juliet* thus :

> An houre before the worshipt Sun,
> Peerde forth the golden window of the East.

Lee also quotes, from the same scene, a parallel which Mr. Murry has since emphasized in his essay, *Shakespeare's Dedication*. The poet's dedications to Southampton lend significance to each use of the word ' dedication ', which always occurs in a metaphorical sense, and always has the underlying meaning of ' love '. Another striking parallel is the couplet :

75

THE VOYAGE TO ILLYRIA

> O she is rich, in bewtie onely poore,
> That when she dies, with bewtie dies her store,

which, *mutatis mutandis*, might almost be the concluding couplet to several of the sonnets. Another parallel, one that shows the transference from the private to the public document which we have already alluded to, occurs at the beginning of Act V. Romeo says :

> If I may trust the flattering truth of sleepe . . .
> I dreamt my Lady came and found me dead . . .
> And Breath'd such life with kisses in my lips,
> That I reuiude and was an Emperor.

This finds its counterpart in *Sonnet* 87 :

> Thus haue I had thee as a dreame doth flatter,
> In sleepe a King, but waking no such matter.

Flattery, as the prelude to disappointment, occurs also in *Sonnet* 33, and a line in the same sonnet sums up the tragedy of Juliet :

> But out alack, he was but one houre mine,
> The region cloude hath mask'd him from me now.

It has, too, the same imagery of the sun.

There are two other points that require brief comment. Romeo, in love with Rosaline, looks forward to Orsino with his sentimental passion for Olivia, and the name Rosaline belongs, also, to the heroine of *Love's Labour's Lost*, where she is described in the same terms. She is drawn from life. Shakespeare's model was the Dark Lady.

A Midsummer Night's Dream was written immediately after *Romeo and Juliet,* though the *New Cambridge* editors (as everywhere) see evidence of subsequent revisions. The Queen Mab speech of Mercutio looks forward to the fairy scenes. Some of Thisbe's lines read like a parody of Juliet's, and, in fact, the Pyramus and Thisbe play is a parody of the tragedy of *Romeo and Juliet.* Mercutio's lines :

> True, I talke of dreames :
> Which are the children of an idle braine,
> Begot of nothing but vaine phantasie

find a parallel in the speech of Theseus :

> Louers, and mad men haue such seething braines,
> Such shaping phantasies,

and another in Puck's :

> This weake and idle theame,
> No more yielding but a dreame.

Miss Spurgeon has described the effect of the imagery in the creation of atmosphere, ' the woodland beauty of the dreaming summer night'. Shakespeare's resources on the stage were so limited that he was compelled to paint his scenery with words, and *A Midsummer Night's Dream* is one of the best examples of his skill. More images are drawn from Nature than in any other early play of his, and the proportion is almost as high as in *Venus and Adonis.*

This fact and the description of the bad weather of 1594 make it likely that the play, or part of it, was written in the country.

Hermia is described as an Ethiope and a tawny Tartar. She is another sketch of the inescapable Dark Lady. The lover, in the speech of Theseus, sees Helen's beauty in a brow of Egypt, and the plot of the play is designed to illustrate Puck's ejaculation, ' Lord, what fooles these mortals bee ! ' The magic employed by Puck and Oberon symbolizes the power of love, its illogicality and unreasonableness, from which not even Titania is immune. Her love for the ass is really the story of Beauty and the Beast, which is itself a fable of love's unreason. It was a theme which continued to interest Shakespeare, for it plays a large part in *Much Ado About Nothing*. The tangle of his own loves would make love at cross-purposes a congenial subject for comedy.

There may be a deeper connection between Shakespeare's own story and the story of the play. The quarrel between Oberon and Titania about the ' louely boy stollen from an Indian king ' may be an imaginative version of the drama of the *Sonnets*, though, in the play, Oberon (Shakespeare) wins the boy. Shakespeare, it is true, had lost the boy of the *Sonnets* to the Dark Lady, but he had later been reconciled to him, and it is reasonable to identify Oberon, the King of the Fairies, the controller of human destinies by the power of imagination, with Shakespeare the dramatist, who gives to airy nothing a local habitation and a name.

The Indian boy was suggested by a reference in *The Metamorphoses*, and the second speech which refers to him echoes the passage from the second Sestiad of *Hero and*

TUTELAGE

Leander quoted in our third chapter, and looks forward
to the first of Ariel's songs :

> His mother was a Votresse of my order :
> And in the spiced *Indian* ayer, by night,
> Full often hath she gossipt by my side,
> And sat, with me on *Neptunes* yellow sands.

It may not be altogether fanciful to see in the Indian boy
the first germ of Ariel.

The Taming of the Shrew need not detain us long. It
appears to be an adaptation by Shakespeare with the
assistance of a collaborator. The most Shakespearean
thing about it is the Induction, with its Warwickshire
reminiscences, Ovidian echoes, its players, who remind us
of *Hamlet*, and the beggar Christopher Sly. For the rest,
we are content to leave it in fitting obscurity.

IV

TUTELAGE

Part II

IV

THERE remain to be considered *Titus Andronicus* and
the early Histories, which are interesting rather as a
revelation of Shakespeare's experiments in technique when
he was learning his job than for the light they throw on his
personality. It is fairly evident that the Histories are more
impersonal than either the comedies or the tragedies, and
the reason is not far to seek. The actual material was too
intractable, the choice of theme too limiting to permit of
much else. As Keats put it :

> Particular facts kept him in the high
> road, and would not suffer him to turn down leafy and
> winding lanes, or to break wildly and at once into the
> breathing fields. The poetry is for the most part ironed
> and manacled with a chain of facts, and cannot get free ; it
> cannot escape from the prison house of history, nor often
> move without our being disturbed with the clanking of
> its fetters.

It is by no means certain that all of *Titus Andronicus* is
by Shakespeare. If it is very early, the versification is
astonishingly mature. If it was written after 1593, then
the other characteristics are unexpectedly feeble. From
Ravenscroft's statement and internal evidence, we are led
to conclude that it was a revision of a play in which Shakespeare was not much interested. The rape theme connects
it with *Lucrece*, written at the same time, and the characterization of Aaron and Tamora is not without power.

THE VOYAGE TO ILLYRIA

There are numerous echoes of Ovid, but these are no proof of authorship, as several of the University wits were fond of Ovid. Nevertheless, Shakespeare's hand would seem to be revealed in certain passages, and Aaron is a forerunner of Iago, particularly in his end.

Part I of *Henry VI* was only partly by Shakespeare. The only certain traces of his hand are in II, iv, and IV, ii. These were, in all probability, added after the writing of the second and third parts, and the most likely assumption is that he began his career as a dramatic author collaborating with Peele in the composition of Part I. Parts II and III are mainly Shakespeare's, and the following passage would seem to have been inserted several years after the completion of the rest :

Shame and Confusion all is on the rout,
Feare frames disorder, and disorder wounds
Where it should guard. O Warre, thou sonne of hell,
Whom angry heauens do make their minister,
Throw in the frozen bosomes of our part,
Hot Coales of Vengeance. Let no Souldier flye.
He that is truly dedicate to Warre,
Hath no self-loue : nor he that loues himselfe,
Hath not essentially, but by circumstance
The name of Valour. O let the vile world end,
And the premised Flames of the Last day,
Knit earth and heauen together.
Now let the generall Trumpet blow his blast,
Particularities, and pettie sounds
To cease. Was't thou ordain'd (deere Father)
To loose thy youth in peace, and to atcheeue
The Siluer Liuery of aduised Age,

And in thy Reuerence, and thy Chaire-dayes, thus
To die in Ruffian battell ? Euen at this sight,
My heart is turn'd to stone : and while 'tis mine,
It shall be stony.   Yorke, not our old men spares :
No more will I their Babes, Teares Virginall,
Shall be to me, euen as the Dew to Fire,
And Beautie, that the Tyrant oft reclaimes,
Shall to my flaming wrath, be Oyle and Flax.

This could not have been written before 1596. It is in
the very rhythm of the later English Histories. It is
equally certain that Shakespeare did not write the Joan of
Arc scenes, though we must not imagine that he ever
conceived of Joan as a saint.

The most interesting passage in the trilogy, apart from
Clifford's speech quoted above, is the parting between
the Queen and Suffolk in Part II. The imagery, like
that of *Romeo and Juliet*, unites the themes of love and
death.

If I depart from thee, I cannot liue,
And in thy sight to dye, what were it else,
But like a pleasant slumber in thy lap ?
Heere could I breath my soule into the ayre,
As milde and gentle as the Cradle-babe,
Dying with mothers dugge betweene it's lips.
Where from thy sight, I should be raging mad,
And cry out for thee to close vp mine eyes :
To haue thee with thy lippes to stop my mouth :
So should'st thou eyther turne my flying soule,
Or I should breathe it so into thy body,
And then it liu'd in sweete Elizium.

THE VOYAGE TO ILLYRIA

To dye by thee, were but to dye in iest,
From thee to dye, were torture more then death :
Oh let me stay, befall what may befall.

The Queen replies :

Away : Though parting be a fretfull corosiue,
It is applyed to a deathfull wound.

The best comment on Suffolk's words is that of Keats :

Now more than ever seems it rich to die,
To cease upon the midnight with no pain.

One of the Shakespearean scenes in the first part has a
typical image which recurs in later plays, that of the stag
at bay :

How are we park'd and bounded in a pale ?
A little Heard of Englands timorous Deere,
Maz'd with a yelping kennell of French Curres.
If we be English Deere, be then in blood,
Not Rascall-like to fall downe with a pinch,
But rather moodie mad : And desperate Stagges,
Turne on the bloody Hounds with heads of Steele,
And make the Cowards stand aloofe at bay.

In his treatment of the Cade scenes, Shakespeare exhibits
his constant scornful dislike of the mob, which showed
itself later in *Sir Thomas More, Julius Caesar, Measure for
Measure,* and *Coriolanus* ; and in Henry's famous soliloquy
in praise of a pastoral life, contrasted with the cares of

office and kingship, we have a forerunner of *Henry IV* and *Henry V*, as well as of *As You Like It* :

> Giues not the Hawthorne bush a sweeter shade
> To Shepheards, looking on their silly Sheepe,
> Then doth a rich Imbroider'd Canopie
> To Kings, that feare their Subiects treacherie ?

But it would seem that Shakespeare did not yet suffer from the insomnia which is manifest in the later plays, or he would have developed the theme here, as he always afterwards did in similar contexts. The scene in which it occurs is a parable on the futility of war, and it is clear that he was more interested in the saintly Henry than in the heroes of the wars.

It is hazardous to attempt to draw any conclusions from the imagery. Plays which may have had several authors, and which were certainly revised, can tell us nothing about Shakespeare's personality, and little about his conception of the theme. We may draw attention, however, to the use of animal symbolism, especially wild beasts and reptiles, tigers, wolves, vipers ; the use of birds of ill-omen so prominent in *Lucrece* and *Macbeth* ; and the frequent Ovidian echoes, not all Shakespeare's.

Edward's wooing of Lady Grey is very similar to the scene in the anonymous *Edward III*, where the King woos the Countess of Salisbury. This contains one quotation from Shakespeare's unpublished *Sonnets* and several unmistakable echoes, a reference to his favourite *Hero and Leander*, and is concerned with the theme of the embassage of love and courtship by proxy which comes in *Much Ado About Nothing*, *Twelfth Night*, and (sadly degraded) in *Troilus and*

G

THE VOYAGE TO ILLYRIA

Cressida. The imagery in the whole of Act II, and in the second scene of Act I is Shakespearean, though Swinburne thought that these scenes were by an imitator, and Sir Edmund Chambers remains unconvinced.

Shakespeare's hand seems to us to be clearly discernible in the following passages, a few examples out of many :

Changing passion like inconstant clouds :
That racke vpon the carriage of the windes,
Increase and die . . .

His cheekes put on their scarlet ornaments,
But no more like her oryentall red,
Then Bricke to Corrall.

To one that shames the faire and sots the wise,
Whose bodie is an abstract or a breefe,
Containes ech generall vertue in the worlde,
Better then bewtifull thou must begin,
Deuise for faire a fairer word then faire,
And euery ornament that thou wouldest praise,
Fly it a pitch aboue the soare of praise.

Her hair far softer then the silke wormes twist,
Like to a flattering glas doth make more faire
The yellow Amber . . .
Ah ! what a world of descant makes my soule,
Vpon this voluntarie ground of loue.

And will your sacred selfe,
Comit high treason against the King of heauen,
To stamp his Image in forbidden mettel ?

TUTELAGE

But O thou world great nurse of flatterie,
Whie dost thou tip mens tongues with golden words,
And peise their deedes with weight of heauie leade,
That faire performance cannot follow promise ?

What can one drop of poyson harme the Sea,
Whose hugie vastures can digest the ill,
And make it loose his operation ?

The freshest summers day doth soonest taint,
The lothed carrion that it seemes to kisse.

      Decke an Ape
In tissue, and the beautie of the robe
Adds but the greater scorne.

That poyson shewes worst in a golden cup,
Darke night seemes darker by the lightning flash.

Lust is a fire, and men like lanthornes show,
Light lust within them selues ; euen through them selues :
Away loose silkes or wauering vanitie,
Shall the large limmit of faire Brittanye,
By me be ouerthrowne, and shall I not,
Master this little mansion of my selfe ;
Giue me an Armor of eternall steele,
I go to conquer kings, and shall I not then
Subdue my selfe, and be my enimies friend,
It must not be.

O periurde beautie, more corrupted Iudge :
When to the great Starre-chamber ore our heads,

THE VOYAGE TO ILLYRIA

The vniuersell Sessions cals to count,
This packing euill, we both shall tremble for it.

Shakespeare must have planned a play on the subject of
Richard III while he was writing *Henry VI*, for the character of Gloucester looks forward to the later play, which
must, in any event, have been begun soon after. It is a
melodrama rather than a tragedy. The psychology is
much cruder than that of several of the early comedies,
but some attempt is made to raise the play to a tragic
plane by showing that Richard's sins come home to roost.
Act IV, scene iv, and the ghosts, if they are Shakespeare's,
were introduced for this purpose. The play, as a whole,
is much more of a unity than any part of the trilogy which
preceded it, and the verse is more mature than all except
the best passages written before. But there is still a com-
parative lack of vital imagery, and this goes to show that
the poet's personality was not deeply engaged. There
are some notable exceptions, but most of the imagery
fails to add to the atmosphere, and gives us little clue to
Shakespeare's unconscious conception of the play.

Some of the exceptions may be noted. Richard, like
Macbeth, cannot sleep. The little princes, like Banquo and
Fleance, are his sweet sleep's disturbers. Like Macbeth,
again, he is in so far in blood that sin will pluck on sin.
Anne is deprived of the golden dew of sleep because of
Richard's dreams, and he begs his supporters not to let
babbling dreams affright their souls. He is troubled by
the worm of conscience, a word that cowards use, devised
to keep the strong in awe. He is referred to by the name
of various obnoxious reptiles and savage beasts, including
the boar, which slew Adonis. His prosperity begins to

mellow and drop into the rotten mouth of death. His mother's womb was a kennel out of which a hell-hound crept. (Compare : ' Turn hell-hound turn.') The course of Justice has wheeled about, and left Elizabeth a very prey to Time. (Compare : ' The wheel is come full circle.') Richard is a foul stone made precious by the foil of England's chair. The All-Seer that Buckingham dallied with has turned his feigned prayer on his head, and gives in earnest what he begged in jest. Sovereignty is an aspiring flame.

Shakespeare's imagination seems to have been kindled by the fate of the little princes. A fine passage describes them :

> girdling one another,
> Within their innocent alablaster armes,
> Their lips were foure red Roses on a stalke,
> Which in their summer beautie kist each other.

This resembles the description of Desdemona on her death-bed. Their mother describes them as her unblown flowers. Their little souls whisper the spirits of Richard's enemies. The phoenix is used as a symbol of the conquest of death by breed :

> In that nest of spicerie they shall breed,
> Selfes of themselues, to your recomfiture.

The most important imagery relates to the sea. Hastings compares him who builds his hope in air of the good looks of the momentary grace of mortal man to a drunken sailor on a mast, ready with every nod to tumble down into the fatal bowels of the deep. Richard says that his greatness is a bark to brook no mighty sea. England is almost shouldered in the swallowing gulf of blind forgetfulness and dark oblivion. Time, in Shakespeare, is often compared to the sea. Queen Elizabeth threatens to anchor her nails in Richard's eyes, and this image suggests another :

> And I in such a desp'rate Bay of death,
> Like a poore Barke, of sailes and tackling reft,
> Rush all to peeces on thy Rocky bosome.

The significance of the sea imagery must be sought in Clarence's dream, where the connexion of disaster at sea with death, one which remained in Shakespeare's mind to the last, is manifest. We have already drawn attention to echoes from *Hero and Leander* in the dream. Shakespeare's gradually evolving attitude to death is of paramount importance in his spiritual development, and, in this speech, death is symbolized as a passing through the sea to reach the dark monarchy of Hell. As we have said, sea and tempest imagery remained with the poet to the end, but, in *The Tempest*, the imagery is expanded into a complete play, and the characters reach the enchanted island instead of Hell. The importance of Clarence's speech finds confirmation in the deepening of the poet's power, and the passage contains some magnificent lines :

> To seeke the emptie vast and wandring aire,

and

TUTELAGE

then came wandring by,
A shadow like an angell, with bright haire
Dabled in blood.

One related consideration remains to be noted, the reference to Julius Caesar, who was already beginning to haunt Shakespeare's mind. Caesar had conquered death :

For now he liues in fame though not in life.

Hastings mocks at Stanley's dreams in much the same way that the conspirator who lures Caesar to the Senate interprets his. The ghosts at the end recall the appearance of Caesar before the battle of Philippi.

Richard II, the last of the experimental Histories, was written about 1595. Shakespeare had now written or helped to write a dozen plays, and the years of his apprenticeship to the University wits were over. He had already passed beyond the range of his masters. If all the powers of Lyly, Greene, and Peele were combined, they could not come within measurable distance of *A Midsummer Night's Dream*, though it may be possible to trace their influence in it. *Romeo and Juliet*, with its tragic pathos, its splendid poetry, and its subtlety of characterization showed how far he had left his teachers behind in tragedy. It was only in the historical play that he had as yet failed to outdistance his predecessors, and we cannot be confident of distinguishing his work from that of his rivals. But the real answer to the disintegrators is twofold. If Shakespeare incorporated in his work scenes from his sources, it was because he felt that they would suit his purpose, and he had an uncanny power of surpassing his predecessors, even when he was avowedly imitating them. In the case of *Richard II*, some of the scenes are so bad that one would willingly believe that Shakespeare was not guilty of writing them, but he was at least guilty of leaving them in.

'It is safest to assume,' writes Sir Edmund Chambers, 'that in the inferior scenes, Shakespeare, completely uninterested in chronicle history, as such, allowed himself to slip into a perfunctory and traditional treatment of all that was not directly concerned with that tragedy.'

Here, Sir Edmund touches on a vital point. Shakespeare, in the Histories, was gradually converting the shapeless and episodic chronicle-play into a well-constructed art-form, sometimes tragedy, sometimes into an entirely new form ; for example, *Henry IV*, which is neither tragedy, comedy, nor even History, but a double play on the triple theme of kingship, rebellion and honour. In the conversion of chronicle into tragedy, Shakespeare was assisted by the example of Marlowe. *Richard III* is the most Marlovian of all his plays, though it was the Marlovian, Machiavellian character of its hero that prevented it from becoming authentic tragedy. Nevertheless, *Richard II* has so many affinities with *Edward II* that it is difficult not to believe that Shakespeare was consciously emulating Marlowe's performance.

A comparison of the two plays brings out the difference between the two poets. Edward's character is so much simpler than Richard's. He is brought down by his love of favourites, while that is only one aspect of Richard's character. He is destroyed by his inability to rule, an inability which springs from his character, which possesses the charm and ineffectiveness of the poetic temperament, as usually conceived, together with a streak of wilfulness and cruelty. Critics of the last century, and even of this, have waxed moral about Richard, and assured us that Bolingbroke, 'the canker', was intended to represent Shakespeare's conception of a good king. But the real theme of the Histories, as Yeats and Masefield have been at pains to point out, is that the most interesting people, the poetic, the saintly, the spiritual, the witty, and the noble, do not make good kings. It is the ordinary, the unscrupulous, the callous man who makes the good king, not the sweet and lovely rose. It cannot possibly be shown that Shakespeare worshipped success. That is an amiable foible of some of his critics. It is Richard's good qualities, quite as much as his vices, that bring him to destruction, and it is the same with Hamlet, Othello and Brutus, not to mention Cordelia, Desdemona and Caesar.

The simplicity of Edward's character and Marlowe's strict concentration on his theme, which even led him to a bare mention of Bannockburn, make the play a greater unity than *Richard II*. There is less relief in it, and a more nearly uniform standard of dramatic competence. Marlowe, moreover, never allows himself to indulge in poetry for its own sake, whereas Shakespeare became so interested in Richard's character that he gave him long poetic speeches which hold up the action, though the reader could not wish them away. Marlowe moves us with pity and terror in his scenes of Edward in prison. Shakespeare refuses to obtain a dramatic effect at the expense of character. Richard is poetic to the end, and in prison he is so absorbed in his thoughts and feelings that we have little time to pity him. The last soliloquy, as Swinburne pointed out, shows the influence of Marlowe

> in the curious trick of selection and transcription of texts for sceptic meditation and analytic dissection. But we see rather more of the poet and less of his creature the man than Marlowe might have given us.

The 'curious trick' is to be found in the opening scene of *Doctor Faustus*.

To other judgments of Swinburne it is less easy to subscribe. Speaking of the deposition scene, he says it need only be compared with its counterpart in *Edward II*

> to show the difference between rhetorical and dramatic poetry, emotion and passion, eloquence and tragedy, life and literature. The young Shakespeare's scene is full to superfluity of fine verses and fine passages ... Marlowe's is from end to end one magnificent model of tragedy, 'simple, sensuous and passionate' ... It is pure poetry and perfect drama : the fancy is finer and the action more life-like than here.

Swinburne is exaggerating the merits of Marlowe's scene, and wilfully shutting his eyes to Shakespeare's purpose. Here, and *Richard II* is unusual in this respect, the poet was primarily concerned with the elaboration of character, the psychology of failure.

Swinburne makes the good point that the motive and meaning of such characters as York, Norfolk and Aumerle is ill-defined and confused, though the characters are important to the scheme of the play, and that Marlowe's

Gaveston and Mortimer 'are far more solid and definite figures'. It is curious that we should have in this play of Shakespeare's that very concentration on a single character which is the chief defect of all Marlowe's plays, *Edward II* itself excepted.

The chief characteristic of the imagery of *Richard II* is the frequent reference to Scripture, and to religion. Blood, like sacrificing Abel, cries even from the tongueless caverns of the earth. We are on the earth where nothing lives but crosses, cares and grief. Richard describes his false friends as damned without redemption, as Judases; and those who show an outward pity at his fall are Pilates. Bolingbroke is damned in the Book of Heaven, because he has broken his oath. England shall be called Golgotha, because of the civil war arising from Richard's deposition. Bolingbroke comes to ope the purple testament of bleeding war. The Queen calls the gardener a second Adam, and asks what Eve, what serpent had suggested to him to make a second fall of cursed man. Richard says Bolingbroke shall not be greater than himself; if he serve God, we'll serve Him too, and be his fellow so. Bolingbroke tells Exton to wander like Cain through the shades of night. The Bishop of Carlisle warns Bolingbroke not to set house against house. Richard says that he has been delivered to his sour cross, and he quotes, 'Come, little ones', and refers to the camel and the needle's eye. Even the name given him at the font is usurped, and the Queen tells him not to kiss the rod. He proposes to resign the crown, and become a palmer or a hermit.

The reason for this imagery must be sought in Shakespeare's conception of the Divine Right of Kings. Rebellion against Richard was a sin against God, and

THE VOYAGE TO ILLYRIA

Shakespeare seems always to have thought that there was a religious sanction in ' order ' and government.

Richard is frequently described as the sun. Just as when the sun fires the proud tops of the eastern pines, and thieves and murderers stand bare and naked, trembling at themselves, so Bolingbroke, declares Richard, will be self-affrighted and tremble at his sin at the approach of his king. The breath of worldly men cannot depose the deputy elected by the Lord. Angels fight on his side. Gaunt admits that Richard is God's anointed deputy. Richard's master, God Omnipotent, is mustering in the clouds armies of pestilence to strike the unborn children of the rebels. Mowbray speaks of Richard's adding an immortal title to his crown. Bolingbroke cries that his divine soul will answer what he has sworn. Gaunt declares that Heaven will rain hot vengeance on the murderers of Gloucester.

Closely connected with this religious imagery are the frequent references to death. Nothing can we call our own but death and that small model of the barren earth which serves as paste and cover to our bones. In the mortal temples of a king, Death keeps his court, infusing him with self and vain conceit as if this flesh were brass impregnable. ' Fight and die ' is death destroying death. Richard is sworn brother to Necessity. Gaunt's inch of taper is nearly burnt, his lamp has almost used up its oil, and his light is wasted by time. His death is like the setting sun and music at the close. Aumerle's words are buried in the grave of his sorrow.

> One of our soules had wandred in the aire,
> Banisht this fraile sepulchre of our flesh.

Death is spoken of as one who gently would dissolve the bands of life.

The imagery gives us, too, an insight into Richard's tragedy. He is described as a young colt. His rash, fierce blaze of riot will soon burn out, for vanity is an insatiate cormorant which preys upon itself. He has failed to keep time in the music of his life. He is corrupted by the caterpillars Bushy, Bagot and Green. His favourites are weeds that must be rooted out. He is misled by flatterers. He is sick in reputation as a result.

The bitterness against flatterers is everywhere manifest in the play, and from the numerous parallels in the *Sonnets* we can be sure that the bitterness was Shakespeare's own. Most of the parallels belong to the group 34–42, and these were probably contemporaneous with *Richard II*, though there are others in 53, 57 and 61. The most obvious is the use of the word ' sour ' coupled sometimes with the word ' cross '. The second group of parallels relates to the obsession with shadows in a special sense. The remaining parallels relate to slander and reputation. The purest treasure mortal times afford is spotless reputation, and that away, men are but gilded loam or painted clay. England is dear for her reputation through the world. Mowbray is pierced to the soul with slander's venomed spear. All these find their echoes in *Sonnets* 36, 70, 96 and 112. The bitterness against flatterers fits in well with Shakespeare's charges against the rival pens, and the reference to dogs easily won to fawn on any man explains why, in subsequent plays, dogs and flatterers so often recur together.

One other passage calls for passing comment, Richard's soliloquy in prison, in which he hammers out a comparison between his prison and the world :

THE VOYAGE TO ILLYRIA

My braine Ile prooue, the female to my soule,
My soule the father, and these two beget
A generation of still-breeding thoughts.

This seems to throw some light on Shakespeare's conception of poetry as the offspring of the union of mind and soul.

King John, from every point of view, is a sad disappointment. It is not so rich in poetry as its predecessor, and there is less dramatic purpose than in any of Shakespeare's Histories. Indeed, a comparison with its source, *The Troublesome Raigne of King John*, shows that the poet missed several opportunities of motivation, and for no apparent reason. The Bastard's quarrel with Austria, so pointless in *King John*, was caused by the latter's treatment of Richard I, whose lion-skin he was wearing. The Bastard's resentment at the marriage of Blanche was actually due to his previous engagement to her. Shakespeare omits all mention of these important facts. A still more serious fault is that, in the source-play, John's death came as the result of his opposition to Rome, while in *King John* it is completely unmotived. Shakespeare, whether from fastidiousness or because anti-catholic propaganda was no longer so fashionable or so topical as it was at the time of the Armada, minimizes the anti-catholic tendencies of his source, and, as a result, it is difficult to know whether John is to be regarded as the defender of the liberties of England, or as the wicked uncle who tries to murder his nephew Arthur.

One reason for the play's artistic failure lies in the fact that it lacks unity. In one act, the Bastard is the chief character ; in another, Constance ; and in a third, Arthur.

TUTELAGE

It would have been possible to write an effective tragedy which portrayed John brought to his death by his championship of nationalism against Rome. A tragedy might have represented the nemesis which overtook the king for his murder of Arthur. A tragedy might even have been made by combining these two themes, but Shakespeare's play remains an aimless chronicle.

The most notable change that Shakespeare made was in Arthur's age. Instead of a philosophic young man in his twenties, we are presented with a young boy, whose sufferings are nicely calculated to arouse our sympathy. Some critics profess to believe that the death of Shakespeare's own little boy, Hamnet, was the reason for the change, but chronology makes this unlikely.

Most of the striking imagery in the play relates to death, some in the lament of Constance for Arthur, and some in John's death-agonies. His pure brain, which some supposed the soul's frail dwelling-house, foretells the ending of mortality. Death, having preyed upon the outward parts, leaves them invisible, and his siege is now against the mind, the which he pricks and wounds with many legions of strange fantasies, which, in their throng and press to that last hold, confound themselves. There is so hot a summer in John's bosom that all his bowels crumble to dust. He is a scribbled form, drawn with a pen upon a parchment, shrivelling up against a fire. None of his courtiers will bid the winter come to thrust its icy fingers in his maw, nor entreat the North to make its bleak winds kiss his parched lips, and comfort him with cold. The tackle of his heart is cracked and burned, and all the shrouds wherewith his life should sail are turned to one thread, one little hair. He is but a clod and module of confounded royalty.

Constance hails death as ' true redress ', amiable, lovely, odoriferous stench, sound rottenness, misery's love, ' I will thinke thou smil'st, And busse thee as thy wife '.

> But now will Canker-sorrow eat my bud,
> And chase the natiue beauty from his cheeke,
> And he will looke as hollow as a Ghost . . .
> And so hee'll dye : and rising so againe,
> When I shall meet him in the Court of heauen
> I shall not know him : therefore neuer, neuer
> Must I behold my pretty *Arthur* more.

The closing speech by the Bastard in Act IV would seem to be an attempt to connect John's downfall with Arthur's death :

> *England* now is left
> To tug and scamble, and to part by th'teeth
> The vn-owed interest of proud swelling State :
> Now for the bare-pickt bone of Maiesty,
> Doth dogged warre bristle his angry crest,
> And snarleth in the gentle eyes of peace . . .
> and vast confusion waites
> As doth a Rauen on a sicke-falne beast,
> The iminent decay of wrested pompe.
> Now happy he, whose cloake and cincture can
> Hold out this tempest.

Another speech of the Bastard's calls for comment, that on ' commodity '. This cynical discourse on gold as the motive-force in men's lives is a commentary on the rest of the play, and, in so far as the play has any unity at all, this is the clue to it.

The Merchant of Venice has a great deal more unity, and the four stories which are so deftly woven together exemplify the theme of the comedy which is twofold. First, it shows the deceptiveness of appearances, and the image of hair taken from the dead to adorn the living recurs in the *Sonnets*.

> All that glisters is not gold,
> Often haue you heard that told.

Gratiano speaks of those reputed wise for saying nothing, and the two lots of the caskets and the rings are variations on the theme of judging by appearances. Bassanio chooses the right casket because he realizes that the world is deceived with ornament. Antonio declares that an evil soul quoting Scripture is

> like a villaine with a smiling cheeke,
> A goodly apple rotten at the hart.
> O what a goodly out-side falshood hath.

Jessica disguises herself in the lovely garnish of a boy. The personal implication of this can be best appreciated by a comparison with the later *Sonnets*.

The second theme is the conflict between justice and mercy, between the letter and the spirit, between hate and love. It was a conflict which Shakespeare was to play over many times before he could view it dispassionately. It is appropriate that Shylock, whose moving principle is hate, and who stands by the letter of the law, should himself be confounded by a quibble, for it emphasizes the overriding

of justice by mercy. Portia had the perfectly sound hold
over Shylock that he had plotted the death of a citizen, but
it would not have been so theatrically effective, nor so
appropriate to the theme to use this defence first.

There can be no doubt that Portia's great speech on the
quality of mercy, which looks forward to *Measure for
Measure*, was intended to be Shakespeare's antithesis to the
hate which governs Shylock. Shylock is the villain, not
the hero, but Shakespeare became so interested in the
character that he made the atrocious villain of a fairy-story
human and even, at times, sympathetic. It is an artistic
error to insert a realistic character in a romantic setting, as
it destroys the harmony of the play. It is difficult to
regret a fault that arose from the breadth of Shakespeare's
sympathies, but it is essential that our own should not be
divided in the trial-scene.

The last act of the play is a masterly creation of atmosphere. It rounds off the play with music :

> The man that hath no musique in himselfe,
> nor is not moued with concord of sweet sounds,
> is fit for treasons, stratagems, and spoiles,
> the motions of his spirit are dull as night,
> and his affections darke as *Erebus* :
> let no such man be trusted.

Shylock, it will be remembered, hates music. Here, as
always, Shakespeare associates music with love, and music
to him, always and increasingly, was the antithesis of hate,
tragedy, and discord.

Portia, with her wit and frankness, her unassuming goodness, her swiftness of purpose, and, above all, her generous

surrender to love, is a worthy forerunner of the great trio of heroines, Beatrice, Rosalind and Viola. Three speeches in one scene bring out the different sides of her character. In the first, when she sees that Bassanio has chosen the right casket, she cries :

> O loue be moderate, allay thy extasie,
> In measure raine thy ioy, scant this excesse,
> I feele too much thy blessing, make it lesse
> for feare I surfeit.

In the second, she surrenders to Bassanio :

> Though for my selfe alone
> I would not be ambitious in my wish
> to wish my selfe much better, yet for you,
> I would be trebled twentie times my selfe.

In the third, she refuses to consummate her marriage till Antonio is saved :

> For neuer shall you lie by *Portias* side
> vvith an vnquiet soule.

Sir Edmund Chambers has pointed that Antonio's melancholy, which would be more appropriate in a tragedy as a premonition of impending disaster, is out of place, and that it preceded the loss of his riches. Bassanio was leaving his friend in order to be married, and Antonio confesses as much to him.

' Consider, again,' continues Sir Edmund, ' the scene

THE VOYAGE TO ILLYRIA

described by Salarino at Bassanio's embarking, still before any question of the miscarriage of his vessels can have come to his ears, how—

> His eyes being big with tears,
> Turning his face, he put his hand behind him,
> And with affection wondrous sensible
> He wrung Bassanio's hand. . . .

'I think he only loves the world for him,' says Salarino. Bassanio was merely voyaging a few miles from Venice, but it was to his wedding, and Antonio knew well how hardly the closest intimacies of bachelors survive the coming of a woman's love . . .

'Consider, too, how in the trial scene he says farewell to his friend :

> Say how I loved you, speak me fair in death :
> And when the tale is told bid her be judge
> Whether Bassanio had not once a love.

I am inclined to doubt whether this particular point in the play was intended for the audience at all, and is not rather the intrusion of a personal note, an echo of those disturbed relations in Shakespeare's private life of which the . . . record is to be found in the *Sonnets*. Shakespeare, too, like Antonio, had lost a friend, and had lost him through a woman ; nor does it seem to me to be inconsistent with any view which Shakespeare can be supposed to have taken of his art, that he should reserve something behind the arras of a play for his own ear, for the secret consolation of his private trouble.'

TUTELAGE

The two parts of *Henry IV* may be regarded in two ways, as a ten-act play on the theme of rebellion, or as two satirical comedies on war and policy. Shakespeare's plays can seldom be tied down to a single purpose. When we come to discuss his views on ' order ', we shall consider the concept of rebellion in *Henry IV*, and its relation to his more private feelings. Here, it need only be said that the King had himself rebelled against Richard II, and he, in turn, is punished with rebellion. But although Bolingbroke, now King, had been a thorn and a canker compared to Richard, the sweet and lovely rose, although he was a politician and a king of smiles, who stole all courtesy from heaven, and plucked allegiance from men's hearts, although the cause of the rebels is just to all appearances, Shakespeare believes that nothing can justify rebellion.

In Henry's first speech, the evils of civil war are powerfully described :

> No more the thirsty entrance of this soile
> Shal dawbe her lips with her own childrens bloud.

Hotspur declares that the rebels wear the detested blot of murderous subornation for supporting Bolingbroke, the ingrate and cankered murderer of Richard. They in the world's wide mouth live scandalized. One of the rebels is described by the King as :

> an exhalde meteor,
> A prodigie of feare, and a portent
> Of broched mischiefe to the vnborne times.

He has faced the garment of rebellion with some fine colour

107

that may please the eye of fickle changelings and poor discontents.

It is sometimes said that the only interest in *Henry IV* is in the unhistorical scenes. This is obviously false. The links between plot and underplot are as close as, for example, in *Twelfth Night*. When Voltaire criticized Shakespeare for his comic underplots, he failed to perceive the dramatic significance of their relationship to the rest of the play. In *Henry IV*, the underplot is a parody of the noble heroics of the main plot. Falstaff, with his army and his views on honour, is the reality : King and rebels, with their statecraft and honour, the fiction he explodes. Shakespeare, with his usual fairness, has left it to the audience's judgment to decide between Falstaff and his betters, but he leaves us in no doubt of his own views. The case has been ably put by Mr. L. C. Knights in his *Notes on Comedy*. For example :

In the battle scene the heroics of ' Now, Esperance, Percy, and set on ' the chivalric embrace are immediately followed by the exposure of a military dodge for the preservation of the king's life ... Satire implies a standard ; and in *Henry IV* the validity of the standard is questioned ; hence the coherence and universality of the play.

In this twilight of hypocrisy, the speech of Prince Hal in which his reformation is forecast reveals him in a lurid and unpleasant light :

Yet herein wil I imitate the sunne,
Who doth permit the base contagious clouds
To smother vp his beautie from the world,

TUTELAGE

That when he please againe to be himselfe,
Being wanted he may be more wondred at . . .
And like bright mettal on a sullein ground,
My reformation glittring ore my fault,
Shal shew more goodly, and attract more eyes
Then that which hath no foile to set it off.

It is worth noting that Shakespeare always regarded the Lancastrians in this way, as calculating creatures, and this is part of their hereditary ingratitude, but the imagery is that of the ' sun ' of the *Sonnets*.

The second part is painted in sombre colours. The Machiavellian policy or treachery of Lancaster which brings about the destruction of the rebels is paralleled by the singularly unpleasant casting-off of the aged Falstaff by the Prince, now King, and the fuller significance of these scenes will appear in the next chapter. The disease *motiv*, already prevalent in the first part, in the second is universal. The diseases of Falstaff and Doll Tearsheet are described in detail. The Lord Chief Justice is senile. Northumberland, feigning illness, is nearly crazed by the death of his son. The King is dying, but cannot sleep till he dies. Shallow is declining into his dotage. Bullcalf pleads that he is a diseased man. He has a whoreson cough caught with ringing in the King's affairs upon his coronation day. Falstaff declares :

A man can no more separate age and couetousnesse, than a can part yong limbs and lechery, but the gowt galles the one, and the pox pinches the other.

With disease, death is linked. Falstaff reproaches Doll :

THE VOYAGE TO ILLYRIA

Peace good Doll, do not speake like a deathes head, do not bid me remember mine end.

Feeble (his name is relevant), addressing Bardolph, says :

We owe God a death . . . He that dies this yeere is quit for the next.

The imagery tells a similar tale.   The Archbishop says :

> Wee are all diseas'd,
> And with our surfetting, and wanton howres,
> Haue brought our selues into a burning Feuer,
> And wee must bleede for it.

The rebels

> did fight with queasinesse, constrain'd
> As men drinke Potions.

On two occasions, the King talks of his kingdom in metaphors of the sick-room :

O my poore kingdome ! sicke with ciuill blowes,

and :

> Then you perceiue the body of our kingdome,
> How foule it is, what rancke diseases grow,
> And with what danger neare the heart of it.

When Falstaff refuses to obey the Lord Chief Justice, he

TUTELAGE

refers to his offence as 'a horson apoplexi'. From the imagery, as from the dramatic themes, the second part of *Henry IV* appears as the most pessimistic play in the canon. There is no heroism or nobility to offset the prevailing gloom :

> Past, and to Come, seemes best ; things Present, worst,

and the King declares that if we could see the revolutions of time :

> The happiest youth viewing his progresse through,
> What perills past, what crosses to ensue ?
> Would shut the booke and set him downe and die.

Northumberland's speech seems to strike the keynote of the play :

> Let heauen kisse earth, now let not Natures hand
> Keepe the wild floud confind, let Order die,
> And let this world no longer be a stage,
> To feed contention in a lingring act :
> But let one spirite of the first borne Cain
> Raigne in all bosomes, that ech heart being set
> On bloudy courses, the rude sceane may end,
> And darkenesse be the burier of the dead.

Shakespeare had reached a period in his life when he believed in nothing, not even in the possibility of nobility. There is no Cordelia, no Kent. Falstaff alone is left, whose massive body bestrides the two plays like a colossus. He is the flesh, graced only with an unparalleled store of wit and humour. What we recognize as disgusting in humanity and in ourselves is in Falstaff made amusing and lovable. He has the courage to admit his vices, even the vice of cowardice. He believes in the survival of the fittest, and the fittest are those who survive. The rest are brave because they dare not be cowards, or because, in his view, they are too stupid to realize that to live is more important than anything else.

In this great, not to say gross, figure, Shakespeare embodied his views of humanity in the years 1597–8. He was tired, and he was able to steer an even course over the seas of life only by throwing overboard the ideals he had set himself in the early plays and the *Sonnets*. He seems to be saying, 'Falstaff, be thou my good'. If those ideals did still exist, it was in reality, not in fact. But we must be just. The verse in *Henry IV* takes a leap forward to maturity. It has more power than in any earlier play, and there is a new skill observable in its employment. So far, blank verse had tended to have a levelling effect on the characters, but now Hotspur has a brittle, spitting verse that is individual, and Glendower's Welsh eloquence springs from the verse he speaks. The creation of Falstaff is undeniably the greatest triumph of Shakespeare's career so far, but one that was in danger of circumscribing his activities, and making him a Molière *malgré lui*. That he perceived the danger himself, may be seen from the way in which he answered the public (perhaps royal) demand, by putting a dummy Falstaff into a farce, and by refusing to allow his reappearance in *Henry V*, though, as we shall show in the next chapter, there was another reason why Falstaff could not appear again.

Henry V, like *King John*, shows patent signs of boredom. The political parts are dull, and lifted straight from *Holin-*

shed's Chronicle ; the patriotic scenes are very weak compared with John of Gaunt's praise of England, and the comic scenes are mostly feeble. Shakespeare's metaphors were becoming forced, a sure sign of weariness, and, from the choruses, it is clear that he was doubting the possibility of exhibiting military glory on the stage. Unconsciously, he was doubting the value of military glory. High hopes of the Essex expedition in Ireland may have given his belief a fresh spur, but he soon learned his lesson. Only two scenes exhibit his full power, that in which the death of Falstaff is announced, and the grave prose discussion concerning the responsibility of war.

V

JOURNEY TO THE PHOENIX

Vna est, quae reparet seque ipsa reseminet, ales;
Assyrii phoenica vocant.

OVID

O blest unfabled incense tree.

DARLEY

I am certain of nothing except the holiness of the
heart's affections.   What the imagination seizes
for beauty must be truth.

KEATS

V

*M*UCH *Ado about Nothing*, the first of the mature comedies of Shakespeare, is inferior to the other two. The Beatrice and Benedick scenes are so realistic that the melodramatic plot is shown up for what it is. Taken alone, Claudio's shaming of Hero in church would pass as an ordinary incident in a romantic play, but as soon as Beatrice applies to it the standards of an intelligent and rational woman, it is revealed as the inexcusable action of a cad, whose subsequent marriage to Hero revolts our ideas of decency.

The Beatrice-Benedick scenes are in prose, and, as in the contemporaneous *Henry IV*, the prose scenes run away with Shakespeare. In *As You Like It*, too, there are indications that Shakespeare was becoming dissatisfied with blank verse as a medium for expressing character. The more vital characters speak in prose. Jaques says to Orlando, ' God buy you an you talk in blank verse ', and Touchstone remarks that the truest poetry is the most feigning.

The theme of *Much Ado about Nothing*, as Mr. Masefield has pointed out, is ' the power of report, of the thing overheard, to alter human destiny '. Both Borachio and Antonio's man overhear Don Pedro's plan to woo Hero for Claudio, though Shakespeare does nothing to make the plan itself credible. Presumably, it was inserted to make more plausible Claudio's subsequent credulity when he watches Borachio making love to ' Hero '. Borachio is overheard by Dogberry and the watch. Benedick over-

hears that Beatrice is in love with him. Beatrice over-
hears that Benedick is in love with her. Everything, in fact,
is sacrificed to the development of the same theme. The
way in which the various plots are dovetailed is masterly,
but, artistically, the play is spoilt by the insertion of realistic
characters who chafe the fabric of the romantic plot.

This theme of the power of report was one with which
Shakespeare was intensely concerned in the *Sonnets*, and
Claudio's bitter conclusion that

> Friendship is constant in all other things,
> Saue in the office and affaires of loue

strikes an all too familiar note to the reader of the *Sonnets*.
Shakespeare, as well as Claudio, had committed

> the flatte transgression of a Schoole-boy, who being
> ouer-ioyed with finding a birds nest, shewes it his com-
> panion, and he steales it.

The play is full of a gently ironical criticism of the
faithlessness of lovers. There is the song :

> Sigh no more ladies, sigh no more,
> Men were deceiuers euer,
> One foote in sea, and one on shore,
> To one thing constant neuer.

There is Beatrice's mockery of the inconstancy of Benedick
in friendship :

> He hath euery month a new sworne brother . . . he

weares his faith but as the fashion of his hat, it euer changes
with the next blocke . . . Is there no yong squarer now
that will make a voyage with him to the diuell ? . . . O
Lord, he will hang vpon him like a disease.

Claudio, too, who has just fallen in love with Hero is so
far uncertain of himself as to say :

> If my passion change not shortly.

Despite Benedick's protests that he will never fall in love,
there are various indications in the play that he has been
something of a rake in the past. This provides one of
Beatrice's main lines of attack, and explains why she is
unwilling to confess her love. Benedick, apparently,
had once made love to her.

> You haue lost the heart of Signior Benedicke.
> Indeed my Lord, he lent it me awhile.

She describes him as a good soldier to a woman, and, in
the first scene, observing Hero, says to Leonato :

> I thincke this is your daughter.

Leonato replies :

> Her mother hath many times tolde me so.

Benedick inquires :

> Were you in doubt sir that you askt her ?

I   119

and Leonato, implying that Benedick has the reputation of a rake, answers :

Signior Benedicke, no, for then you were a child.

Beatrice is a more subtle version of the Shrew.

There is a character of the stage-directions who fails to materialize, ' Innogen ', the mother of Hero. It may be recalled that *Cymbeline* was known to the Jacobeans as ' Innogen ', and it is interesting to examine the resemblance in plot between *Much Ado About Nothing* and *Cymbeline*. In both, much turns on the purity of a woman, and, in each case, false evidence is concocted to ruin her reputation and good name. The plot, in each case, is foiled, and death retreats, but between these two plays comes *Othello*, where a similar plot succeeds, and the heroine dies. When Shakespeare was writing *Much Ado About Nothing*, he was still able to feel that such purity existed, and could survive, but with the tragedies, that feeling of certainty went, and it was not until the Romances that he recovered the faith he asserted in *Much Ado About Nothing*.

Critics have attempted to infer from the titles *As You Like It* and *Twelfth Night or What You Will* that Shakespeare was contemptuously giving the public what it wanted. But masterpieces are not written in that mood, and one has only to compare his genuine pot-boilers, *The Taming of the Shrew* and *The Merry Wives of Windsor* with *Twelfth Night*, to see the difference. It is true that *As You Like It* is carelessly written, that the opening is one of Shakespeare's feeblest, that the ending is slipshod, and, as Johnson said :

JOURNEY TO THE PHOENIX

By hastening to the end of his work Shakespeare suppressed the dialogue between the usurper and the hermit, and lost an opportunity of exhibiting a moral lesson in which he might have found matter worthy of his highest powers.

Nor does the play get under way until the characters have been shepherded to the Forest of Arden. The witty dialogue between Rosalind and Celia in the second scene of the first act is as forced and artificial as one of Lyly's, but as soon as Rosalind dons doublet and hose, the play becomes alive. One can only assume that the play was written in the haste of inspiration, and denied even the cursory revision of re-reading by a sudden call for performance.

Shakespeare's desire to leave London, and return to Stratford, where he had just bought the largest house, may be expressed in the Arden scenes. He was tired of the artificiality, ' the painted pomp', of the city and the court. But he realized that this desire to get away into the country was largely a desire to escape from himself, and he knew that Stratford was not the Arden his memory sometimes painted :

I, now am I in *Arden*, the more foole I, when I was at home I was in a better place, but Trauellers must be content.

As soon as the courtiers have the opportunity to return to civilization, only the melancholy Jaques refuses.

In the character of Jaques, who, it must be remembered, was a creature of Shakespeare's own invention—he is not in the novel from which the plot was drawn—the poet is considering his own function as a comic dramatist.

THE VOYAGE TO ILLYRIA

                    I must haue liberty
Withall, as large a Charter as the winde,
To blow on whom I please, for so fooles haue :
And they that are most gauled with my folly,
They most must laugh . . .
Inuest me in my motley : Giue me leaue
To speake my minde, and I will through and through
Cleanse the foule bodie of th'infected world,
If they will patiently receiue my medicine.

It is Jaques, too, who moralizes on the theme of 'All the
world's a stage'. The detached interest he takes in the
love-affairs of Orlando and Touchstone, and his parting
words to the various characters in the last scene of the play
represent the part that Shakespeare himself was playing.

But Shakespeare also satirizes his own melancholy.
Rosalind says she would rather have a fool to make her
merry, than experience to make her sad, and the Duke
declares that Jaques has been a libertine

    As sensuall as the brutish sting it selfe.
    And all th'imbossed sores, and headed euils,
    That thou with license of free foot hast caught,
    Would'st thou disgorge into the generall world.

The satire of the play has many facets. The affectations
of the court are satirized by the juxtaposition of the Forest
of Arden, and the pastoral of the exiled courtiers is shown
in its true colours by the picture of the country 'as it
really is' in the person of the slut Audrey. Touchstone
and Jaques are admirably balanced, and the courtship of
Rosalind and Orlando is played against the background

of the affairs of Phebe and Silvius, and of Touchstone and
Audrey.

Phebe, from her description, would seem to be own
sister to Rosaline, and the other women whose model was
the Dark Lady of the *Sonnets*. Shakespeare, avenging his
injuries for the last time, attacks her through the mouth
of Rosalind.

> What though you haue no beauty
> As by my faith, I see no more in you
> Then without Candle may goe darke to bed :
> Must you be therefore prowd and pittilesse ? . . .
> 'Tis not your inkie browes, your blacke silke haire,
> Your bugle eye-balls, nor your cheeke of creame
> That can entame my spirits to your worship . . .
> Sell when you can, you are not for all markets.

We may compare the description in the *Sonnets* :

> Therefore my Mistersse eyes are Rauen blacke,
> Her eyes so suted, and they mourners seeme,

or :

> My Mistres eyes are nothing like the Sunne,
> Currall is farre more red, then her lips red,
> If snow be white, why then her brests are dun :
> If haires be wiers, black wiers grow on her head.

The resemblance is unmistakable.

In a later scene, Rosalind chides Silvius for loving Phebe :

> Wilt thou loue such a woman ? what to make thee an

instrument, and play false straines vpon thee ? not to be endur'd.

Rosalind herself is called Ganymede, and we have here the paradoxical situation of the *Sonnets* again dramatized.

The imagery creates the pastoral atmosphere of the play, and paints the corrupt world from which the courtiers have escaped. Exiled in Arden, they find that sweet are the uses of adversity, which, like the toad ugly and venomous, wears yet a precious jewel in his head. They escape from the workaday world full of briers, and, despite the icy fang and churlish chiding of the winter's wind, they are able to smile and say, ' This is no flattery '. The bitter sky does not bite so nigh as benefits forgot. They have escaped from a world where fat and greasy citizens refuse to lend a helping hand to the poor and broken bankrupt, where none will sweat but for promotion, where what is comely envenoms him that bears it, and unregarded age is in corners thrown.

Twelfth Night is an exquisite satire on different types of sentimentality, from the Olivia-on-a-pedestal love of Orsino to the Patience-on-a-monument love of Viola, from the unreal grief of Olivia for her brother to the self-regard of Malvolio, from Antonio's worship of Sebastian (But O how vile an idol proves this god !) to Sir Toby's marriage to a serving-maid as her reward for gulling Malvolio. Feste acts as the commentator :

> This fellow is wise enough to play the foole,
> And to do that well, craues a kinde of wit :
> He must obserue their mood on whom he iests,

JOURNEY TO THE PHOENIX

The quality of persons, and the time :
And like the Haggard, checke at euery Feather
That comes before his eye.

His wit is directed against all the main characters of the play, though his irony at Orsino's expense is so cunningly veiled that it passes unnoticed.

The ' barful strife ', set in motion by Viola's disguising herself as Cesario, enables Shakespeare once more to dramatize one aspect of the story of the *Sonnets*, and also to inveigh against ingratitude and faithlessness, a theme which has begun already to intrude even into the sunniest of his comedies.

Antonio reproaches Viola whom he mistakes for Sebastian :

Thou hast *Sebastian* done good feature, shame.
In Nature, there's no blemish but the minde :
None can be call'd deform'd, but the vnkinde.
Vertue is beauty, but the beauteous euill
Are empty trunkes, ore-flourish'd by the deuill,

and Orsino, calling Cesario a dissembling cub, asks bitterly :

What wilt thou be
When time hath sow'd a grizzle on thy case ?

Viola declares that

Nature, with a beauteous wall
Doth oft close in pollution,

and she comments on Olivia's sudden awakening :

125

THE VOYAGE TO ILLYRIA

How easie is it, for the proper false
In womens waxen hearts to set their formes.

Love alone is high fantastical. Orsino admits, first, that
men's fancies are more giddy and unfirm, more longing,
wavering, sooner lost and won than women's are, and then
he says that women

> lacke retention.
> Alas, their loue may be call'd appetite,
> No motion of the Liuer, but the Pallat,
> That suffer surfet, cloyment and reuolt,
> But mine is all as hungry as the Sea,
> And can digest as much.

The connexion between ' love ' and ' hunting ' forms
the most interesting set of images in the play.

Curio.   Will you go hunt my Lord ?
Duke.   What *Curio* ?
Curio.   The Hart.
Duke.   Why so I do, the Noblest that I haue . . .
          That instant was I turn'd into a Hart,
          And my desires like fell and cruell hounds,
          Ere since pursue me.

He is recalling the fate of Actæon who pursued the chaste
Artemis, and he goes on to wonder how Olivia will love,

> when the rich golden shaft
> Hath kill'd the flocke of all affections else
> That liue in her.

126

The connexion dates back to the hunting-love themes of *Venus and Adonis*. It is cemented by the ' heart-hart ' pun, and reinforced by the double sense of the word ' venery ', which means both ' hunting ' and ' the physical expression of sex '.

In the previous chapter, we traced the development of Shakespeare's attitude to death down to the end of the century. The idea of death was naturally associated in his mind with the irreparable ravages of time, and in the *Sonnets*, especially, he declared that there were two ways of conquering death and time, by marriage and breed, or by the immortalizing power of art. We have seen that, in the last years of the century, he had lost his faith in the absolutes in which he had once believed, beauty, truth and goodness. Silvia, in *The Two Gentlemen of Verona*, was holy, fair and wise in the eyes of love, and it is love which converts these absolutes from abstractions into realities. That, as we have shown, was the significance of the imagery of *Romeo and Juliet*. When he wrote that play, love was Shakespeare's religion. It is also the religion expressed in the *Sonnets*. When, therefore, in the profound pessimism of 2 *Henry IV*, Shakespeare revealed his loss of faith in life, it was because he was losing or had already lost his faith in love.

Either he must recover his lost faith, or he will continue to write bad imitations of his early work, all the more barren because they exhibit a more dexterous technique. The plays that followed were his three finest comedies, and *Julius Caesar*, the first of the great tragedies. We must infer, therefore, that by some means, by some experience, he had achieved a new faith in life. He must have undergone some mystical experience which transformed him from the best of the Elizabethans to the Shakespeare we all know. If we had no evidence to go upon, we could safely infer that this experience was concerned with the conquest of death and time, and with the reaffirmation of his belief in love. If we had no record, so much would be certain. The record we have, in *The Phoenix and the Turtle*, a poem which has suffered at the hands of most Shakespearean critics a strange neglect. Doubtless the obscurity of its language has contributed very largely to this, and Professor Carleton Brown expressed accepted opinion when he said : ' Shakespere's brief poem in itself presents a hopeless enigma.' But the impression still remains that the poem is heavily charged with meaning, and it is our purpose to attempt a solution by means of the clues that Shakespeare has so freely dispersed throughout the rest of his work.

The Phoenix and the Turtle appeared in 1601 as one of the additional poems in *Love's Martyr*, but despite this, it is an occasional poem the occasion of which is unknown. For, although Chester's poem, from which the collection took its name, was apparently written some years before, in celebration of the love of his patron Sir John Salusbury and his wife, and ' its mystical reinforcement on the occasion of the birth of their first child ', the other contributions are only superficially related to *Love's Martyr*.

Hereafter follow diuerse poeticall essaies on the former subiect ; viz : the Turtle and Phoenix. Done by the best and chiefest of our moderne writers, with their names subscribed to their particular workes : neuer before extant. And (now first) consecrated by them all generally, to the loue and merite of the true-noble Knight, Sir Iohn Salisburie.

JOURNEY TO THE PHOENIX

The *Vatum Chorus* declare that Salusbury's merits were parents to their several rhymes ; but although Salusbury was a generous patron, and his son wrote commendatory verses to Heminge and Condell on the publication of the *First Folio*, most of the additional poems are independent exercises in the symbolism of the phoenix and the turtle. Shakespeare's poem, in particular, strikes an elegiac note that is alien to its environment, and his birds who leave no posterity are obviously not Sir John and Lady Ursula Salusbury. Sir Sidney Lee even went so far as to say that ' the internal evidence scarcely justifies the conclusion that Shakespeare's poem . . . was penned for Chester's collection '. This is hardly true. It is fairly evident, from the use he makes of the symbolism of the phoenix and the turtle that Shakespeare, like Jonson, Chapman and Marston, had at least glanced at *Love's Martyr*.

A few critics have doubted the authenticity of the poem, and, in a monograph published a few years ago, ' Ranjee ' suggested that John Fletcher was the real author. None of his arguments against Shakespeare's authorship will stand serious consideration, and he offers no valid evidence on behalf of Fletcher. His citation of parallel passages proves only that Fletcher had read the poem, and his admission that it has a maturity impossible to a man of twenty-five vitiates his entire argument. Actually, Fletcher was only twenty-two when *Love's Martyr* appeared, and, furthermore, it is unlikely that a circle in which, for example, Ben Jonson's own MSS. circulated, would either attempt or suffer deception in such an attribution of authorship, whatever an unscrupulous publisher might do. Internal evidence, therefore, will but confirm what was certain already.

THE VOYAGE TO ILLYRIA

The immediate reason for its composition was doubtless a positive request, and the contents of the volume invite (as Mr. W. R. Parker has pointed out to us) comparison with the volume compiled in memory of Edward King. 'J. H.' and 'C. B.' address King's sister, Samson Briggs is almost riddled 'into Atheism' by King's death, and Milton, setting out to celebrate the memory of a friend, actually gives us in *Lycidas* a piece of autobiography.

The broad and superficial outline of *The Phoenix and the Turtle* is not difficult to trace. We have various birds summoned to join in the obsequies of two loyal and faithful birds, the phoenix and the turtle. The birds summoned are birds of good omen, or, more curiously, chaste but of ill omen. The fidelity of the dead birds had been a source of wonder and admiration, so close were the links that joined them. Reason, marvelling, but not comprehending, made the lament over their ashes. It is in the closer interpretation of the poem that critics, as we have already seen, confess themselves baffled. 'Ranjee' rightly disagrees with the late Professor Herford, who called it 'a pleasant jest', and with Grosart, who indulged in a farrago about Elizabeth and Essex, but his own interpretation on the basis of the work of emblematists like Gabriello Simeoni and Arnold Freitag seems to us totally mistaken. Only Mr. Murry, in the essay on poetry in *Discoveries*, appears to have come within striking distance of the problem. Our own attempt, made independently, resembles his in some respects, though it has important differences.

It is clear, we have said, that Shakespeare had glanced at *Love's Martyr*, but there was another book, *The Phoenix Nest*, published in 1593, the contents of which were certainly in his mind. In Matthew Roydon's elegy on Sir Philip

JOURNEY TO THE PHOENIX

Sidney there is a passage of some importance. The author describes the mourners at the funeral thus :

> The skie bred Egle roiall bird,
> Percht there vpon an oke aboue,
> The Turtle by him neuer stird,
> Example of immortall loue.
>   The swan that sings about to dy,
>   Leauing Meander stood thereby.
>
> And that which was of woonder most,
> The Phoenix left sweete Arabie.

This coincidence is not fortuitous, since the line in Shakespeare's poem, 'Death is now the *Phoenix* nest ', suggests another link. Furthermore, the idea of chastity is the subject of a subsequent poem in the same book, and, in ' An excellent Dialogue between Constancie and Inconstancie ' which comes immediately after it, we have a reference to ' loue, which is for the most part, reason beyond reason '. It seems natural to suppose that this is the ' source ' of ' Loue hath Reason, Reason none '.

We have now to discover the idea in Shakespeare's mind which attracted to itself all these fragments, which are related, in their original setting, only by their proximity. In view of what we propose to establish later on, we can say that *The Phoenix and the Turtle* came not long after the final break with Southampton. It must be emphasized that this break is not to be confused with the estrangement mentioned in the *Sonnets* themselves, but was a deeper and more disturbing one, which came after the last sonnet had been written. Despite this, the poem is not one of despair,

131

but of quiet assurance. ' Hope creates From its own wreck
the thing it contemplates.' Therein lies its significance.
Southampton had destroyed the love for which the poet
had been willing to sacrifice everything. ' Take all my
loues, my loue, yea take them all', and Shakespeare now
proclaims that though their mutual love is ended in the
actual world, it exists for ever in eternity. This may be
thought a poor consolation, a sentimental brooding over
what might have been ; but this is to misunderstand the
poem's significance. Though love has been betrayed
brutally, even sordidly, the fact that it once existed is
sufficient assurance to the poet that ' Loue hath Reason',
that is to say is an absolute. He will not admit, as he
afterwards did in a moment of bitterness, that love's betrayal
is a proof that it never existed. Here, he re-enunciates the
testament he wrote when he suspected that Southampton's
affection was cooling :

> Loue is not loue
Which alters when it alteration findes,
Or bends with the remouer to remoue.
O no, it is an euer fixed marke
That lookes on tempests and is neuer shaken ;
It is the star to euery wandring barke,
Whose worths vnknowne, although his higth be taken.
Lou's not Times foole, though rosie lips and cheeks
Within his bending sickles compasse come,
Loue alters not with his breefe houres and weekes,
But beares it out euen to the edge of doome.

Though ' Loue and Constancie is dead', the miracle of
perfect love exists in eternity,

JOURNEY TO THE PHOENIX

> *Phoenix* and the *Turtle* fled,
> In a mutuall flame from hence,

so great was their love on earth.

We come now to the more metaphysical parts of the poem, where the problems are of a different order. Let us take the stanzas that express the unity in disunity of the two birds :

> So they loued as loue in twaine,
> Had the essence but in one,
> Two distincts, Diuision none,
> Number there in loue was slaine.
>
> Hearts remote, yet not asunder ;
> Distance and no space was seene,
> Twixt this *Turtle* and his Queene ;
> But in them it were a wonder.

Shakespeare had already expressed this view of his love in *Sonnet* 36, addressed to Southampton :

> Let me confesse that we two must be twaine,
> Although our vndeuided loues are one.

It was this feeling of the unity of the spirit that enabled Shakespeare to preserve an ultimate faith in love and beauty, even in the Inferno through which he was to pass. Cordelia would be impossible without the emotional conviction expressed in *The Phoenix and the Turtle*. As Mr. Murry so eloquently puts it :

THE VOYAGE TO ILLYRIA

By reason of the mutual disaster which is to engulf them, Lear and Cordelia are lifted up into the condition of *The Phoenix and the Turtle*. Lear's very words : ' We two will sing alone like birds i' the cage ', contain a trembling mortal echo of their song, and Reason might chant over Cordelia the dirge it chanted over them.

Julius Caesar is the first of the tragedies to be ' illuminated by the splendour of the vision ', and this brief poem, written during the same period, is the first expression of that vision. In it, the seed of all Shakespeare's later development is contained. Professor Wilson Knight, in his essay, *The Shakespearian Aviary*, has attempted to show that the symbolism of the first six stanzas[1] can be referred to a particular play. But this is to consider too curiously for our purpose. All we would claim is that the mourners at the obsequies are ' heraulds sad ' of the ' tragique scene ' on to which the poet was about to enter, and that the essence of Shakespearean tragedy is the conflict between the vision and life as we know it. It is clear that when the poem was written, Shakespeare had a prophetic understanding of the experience he must undergo. Shakespearean tragedy is, in a very real sense, the tragedy of Shakespeare himself.

As we can gather from the *Sonnets*, for example, the idea of sex was tarnished for the poet, and he still clung to the

---

[1] Professor Knight connects the various stanzas as follows :— i, *Romeo and Juliet*; ii, *Macbeth*; iii, *Cymbeline*; iv, *The Merchant of Venice*; v, *Hamlet*; vi, *Antony and Cleopatra*; but *Othello* would surely be a better parallel to stanza iv. *Romeo and Juliet* is the only play written before 1600. We might interpret this by saying that it was a forerunner of the tragic period to which the death of love and constancy gave rise, or, alternatively, that the true parallel to stanza i is *Antony and Cleopatra*.

ideal of the marriage of true minds, chaste, and therefore

> Leauing no posteritie,
> Twas not their infirmitie,
> It was married Chastitie.

The poem is a recognition that this love, divorced from its original object, is the motive force behind all his poetry (' So oft haue I inuok'd thee for my Muse '—*Sonnet* 78) ; and it marks the transformation of the lovely boy into the spirit of Ariel.   The validity of this love is next established :

> Truth may seeme, but cannot be,
> Beautie bragge, but tis not she.

It was not Truth, for Truth had been betrayed.   It was not Beauty, for the Beauty he had worshipped played him false.   The answer comes in a brief couplet :

> Loue hath Reason, Reason none,
> If what parts, can so remaine.

Love, it was, to which the others were subsumed, that inspired Shakespeare's plays, a love that would be eventually extended to embrace the whole world.   He had not reached that state, but already his prophetic soul looked forward to the ultimate synthesis, the emotional serenity of *The Tempest.* He looked forward to the time when even Reason would recognize that Love was above Reason.   As Arviragus in *Cymbeline* says :

> I know not why
> I loue this youth, and I haue heard you say,
> Loue's reason's, without reason.

Though ' in itself confounded ', it was Reason that made the threne in honour of the co-supremes and stars of love.

About eight years were to pass before Shakespeare was able to embody these co-supremes in a play, but it was no longer a chaste union. The fidelity was founded on sexual love. The proclamation that ' Loue hath Reason, Reason none ' foreshadows *Antony and Cleopatra*. To Reason, and, alas, to Sir Arthur Quiller-Couch, *Antony and Cleopatra* is *All for Lust*, and Antony sacrifices his honour for the sake of a harlot. To Shakespeare, that actuality was a ludicrous distortion of the reality behind it. He, like the priests, blessed Cleopatra when she was riggish, and Antony is hailed as the Arabian bird. It is noteworthy, too, that bird imagery is more frequent in this play than in any other.

But we must revert to the poem. Truth and Beauty had been set side by side by the poet in *Sonnet* 14. Addressing the lovely boy, he had said, ' Thy end is Truthes and Beauties doome and date ', and so now

> Truth may seeme, but cannot be,
> Beautie bragge, but tis not she,
> Truth and Beautie buried be.

This must not be taken to imply physical death so much as the admission of the power of Death which faithlessness brings in its train, just as fidelity, by its very existence, conquers Death.

This consideration brings us to the problem of why Shakespeare chose the symbolism of the Phoenix to express this determining experience of his life. The Phoenix has been, from time immemorial, a symbol of immortality and resurrection, and Shakespeare's aching desire to overcome the iniquity of oblivion, so manifest in the *Sonnets*, here finds relief :

> Deuouring time blunt thou the Lyons pawes,
> And make the earth deuoure her owne sweet brood,
> Plucke the keene teeth from the fierce Tygers yawes,
> And burne the long liu'd Phænix in her blood.

The immortal Phoenix must make this concession to Time. She must burn in a flame of love, and hence, the bird is a love symbol. In Lyly's *Euphues* and Ovid's *Metamorphoses*, the legend is briefly related, and Golding renders Ovid thus :

> One bird there is that dooth renew itself and as it were
> Beget it self continually. The Syrians name it there
> A *Phœnix*. Neyther corne nor herbes this *Phœnix* liueth
>   by,
> But by the iewce of frankincence and gum of *Amomye*.

Shakespeare doubtless took the idea of the turtle as the devoted mate of the Phoenix from Chester's own poem, *Love's Martyr*, the turtle being, of course, the Paphian dove of Venus.

The Phoenix, finally, is a symbol not only of immortality, but also of death, and the emphasis on death and mourning is a parallel to the thoughts of death in *Julius Caesar* and *Hamlet*. Shakespeare, at the turn of the century, stood on the threshold of the tragic period. The experience which finds expression in the poem enabled him to endure to the end. Love was the star that enabled his 'wandring barke' to survive the 'tempest'. In the plays that follow upon this new attitude, notably *Antony and Cleopatra* and *King Lear*, his concept of order in the Universe is expressed as a belief in constancy and faithfulness, a constancy and faithfulness that, in the tragedies, receives death as its reward, and is the antithesis of the betrayal that compassed the death of Caesar. Years later, Imogen, 'alone the Arabian bird', escaped the normal penalty for constancy, though she had a funeral, and, in *The Tempest*, Prospero's enemies are compelled to admit that

> In *Arabia*
> There is one Tree, the Phœnix throne, one Phœnix
> At this houre reigning there.

When the validity of the vision of *The Phoenix and the Turtle* had been acknowledged, the poet's task was done.

That, then, is the significance of *The Phoenix and the Turtle*. When Shakespeare finished *Henry V* and *The Merry Wives of Windsor*, he had reached a crucial moment in his career as a dramatist. Both plays were inferior to *Henry IV*. It was, as Mr. Masefield puts it, 'slack water' with him. 'The personality was worn to a husk.'

Now artists of all kinds exist and progress by destroying those selves of them which, having flowered, have served. They are continually sitting in judgment upon themselves, and annihilating their pasts by creating opposites.

For this self-annihilation to take place, some change in the artist's life must occur. It may be quite unconnected with his art, except in so far as his art must constitute a selection of his experience. The nature of this change, based on a betrayal of some magnitude, will be best examined in the next chapter. All we need say here is that it occurred before the completion of *Henry IV*, and that, at first, its very magnitude prevented Shakespeare from assimilating it into his art. That is the primary cause of the thinness in texture of the plays that immediately followed. It is an inadequate explanation to assume that they were written to order. In a sense, all his plays were written under the same conditions. They were limited by the requirements of his patrons, even when they most obviously expressed the poet's own personality, but in the plays that followed *Henry IV*, Shakespeare dared not, and, indeed, could not, utter what was nearest his heart. In *Much Ado About Nothing*, which came soon after, apart from the plot against Hero, there is little of the new outlook, but in *As You Like It* the imagery is impregnated with the betrayal theme. It was not, however, until *Julius Caesar*, that Shakespeare faced his experience, and, in doing so, produced a play greater than any he had so far written. The confidence gained by the consciousness of achievement, and the detachment that followed on the writing of the play, enabled him to over-come the bitterness of betrayal. It was a noble achievement, one that required not only the courage of acceptance, but also the power of refusing to generalize from his own misfortunes, but the effects of the victory were short-lived. Either before or just after *The Phoenix and the Turtle*, Shakespeare wrote one supreme comedy, *Twelfth Night*, his loveliest and most perfect, so wise, so tender, in its treatment of human frailty, using such gentle irony against self-deceivers, that the less perceptive critics have failed to observe how delicate was the balance of this fine equilibrium. Cast adrift from Southampton, the poet had to make a further journey, and the tragedies chart the voyage. He had seen Illyria in the setting sun, but night came on, and the tempest of his soul.

VI

BETRAYAL

*He's mad that trusts in the tameness of a wolf, a horses
health, a boys loue, or a whores oath.*

THE FOOL *in* KING LEAR

VI

*J*ULIUS *CAESAR* came at the turning-point of Shakespeare's dramatic career, and it is noteworthy that
three characters are made to say that they have changed
their views. Calphurnia addresses her husband thus :

> *Cæsar*, I neuer stood on Ceremonies,
> Yet now they fright me.

Of the hero it is said :

> For he is Superstitious growne of late,
> Quite from the maine Opinion he held once,
> Of Fantasie, of Dreames, and Ceremonies.

Cassius, in the fifth act, confesses thus :

> You know, that I held *Epicurus* strong,
> And his Opinion : Now I change my minde,
> And partly credit things that do presage.

The inference seems to be that Shakespeare had changed
his own view of omens. In *Sonnet* 107 he had commented
on the false omens :

> Not mine owne feares, nor the prophetick soule,
> Of the wide world, dreaming on things to come,
> Can yet the lease of my true loue controule,
> Supposde as forfeit to a confin'd doome.

THE VOYAGE TO ILLYRIA

The mortall Moone hath her eclipse indur'de,
And the sad Augurs mock their owne presage,
Incertenties now crowne them-selues assur'de,
And peace proclaimes Oliues of endlesse age.
Now with the drops of this most balmie time,
My loue lookes fresh, and death to me subscribes,
Since spight of him Ile liue in this poore rime,
While he insults ore dull and speachlesse tribes.

Now, he has proved them true, and we must examine the working-out of that discovery.

In our second chapter, we drew attention to the fact that Shakespeare particularly identified himself with Julius Caesar. Over a long period of time, he was haunted by the thought of Caesar's greatness, believing him to be the noblest man that ever lived in the tide of time, and there was a very special reason why the subject of Caesar's assassination would appeal to him in 1600. It was Caesar's angel, Brutus, who was the chief conspirator, and Shakespeare had been betrayed by his angel, Southampton. The nature of the betrayal is immaterial; it was not, in all probability, connected with the Dark Lady. What matters far more is that from 1598 onwards ingratitude and betrayal are the leading motives in Shakespeare's work. There are hints of it in *As You Like It*.

Blow, blow, thou winter winde,
Thou art not so vnkinde, as mans ingratitude
Thy tooth is not so keene, because thou art not seene,
    although thy breath be rude.
Heigh ho, sing heigh ho, vnto the greene holly,

BETRAYAL

Most frendship, is fayning ; most Louing, meere folly :
  Then heigh ho, the holly,
  This Life is most iolly.

Freize, freize, thou bitter skie that dost not bight so nigh
  as benefitts forgot :
Though thou the waters warpe, thy sting is not so sharpe,
  as freind remembred not.
    Heigh ho, sing, &c.

Compare these lines with Orlando's poem, where he speaks

  of violated vowes,
    twixt the soules of friend, and friend.

Orlando, describing Rosalind's perfection, says :

  Therefore heauen Nature charg'd,
    that one bodie should be fill'd
  With all Graces wide enlarg'd,
    nature presently distill'd
  Helens cheeke, but not his heart,
    Cleopatra's Maiestie.

 Editors, naturally, emend the *his* of the last line but one to *her*, since the answer to the question, ' Whose heart ? ' is ' Helen's ', but this involves no explanation of the origin of the erroneous gender. Helen's cheek was not a new image to Shakespeare. In an attempt to describe Southampton's perfection, he had recourse to the same method as Orlando. In *Sonnet 53*, it was employed thus :

THE VOYAGE TO ILLYRIA

Describe *Adonis* and the counterfet,
Is poorely immitated after you,
On *Hellens* cheeke all arte of beautie set,
And you in *Grecian* tires are painted new . . .
    In all externall grace you haue some part,
    But you like none, none you for constant heart.

When Shakespeare was writing *As You Like It*, the ' constant
heart ' was constant no more, and his thoughts tricked
him into an unconscious utterance of his sorrow. As we
had already said, before we chanced on this curious error,
it is in such incidental passages as the songs that Shakespeare's
own feelings are most likely to emerge. It may be recalled
that there is a tradition, emanating from Shakespeare's
own brother, that the poet played the part of the faithful
Adam himself.

In *Twelfth Night*, a play which yet shows a greater balance
and serenity than any that followed it during the next eight
years, there is a great deal of discussion of ingratitude.
Viola, for instance, when she is reproached by Antonio
for what were Sebastian's ' offences ' declares :

I hate ingratitude more in a man,
Then lying, vainnesse, babling drunkennesse,
Or any taint of vice, whose strong corruption
Inhabites our fraile blood.

Antonio ' adores ' Sebastian (the word is Shakespeare's),
and when he reproaches Viola for the second time, his
utterance is, perhaps, the most deeply felt in the whole
play :

146

BETRAYAL

His life I gaue him, and did thereto adde
My loue without retention, or restraint,
All his in dedication. For his sake,
Did I expose my selfe (pure for his loue).

Mr. Murry has analysed, in a brilliant essay, Shakespeare's
use of the word ' dedication ', and though we feel bound to
disagree with him in certain crucial details, we have no
doubt that he has demonstrated conclusively, from the
varying contexts of the words ' dedicate ' and ' dedication ',
that the young man of the *Sonnets* was Southampton, and
also that his betrayal was a crisis in Shakespeare's life. In
our final chapter we shall show, as Professor Wilson
Knight has suggested in his *Myth and Miracle*, that
Southampton's betrayal of Shakespeare occurred twelve
years before *The Tempest*. If we date that play 1610, the
betrayal took place about the year 1598. If we were to
accept Professor Leslie Hotson's theory that 2 *Henry IV* was
written in 1597, we could only assume that Shakespeare
was not adhering to mathematical accuracy ; for the
betrayal must have happened before that play was
finished.

Two of the scenes in 2 *Henry IV* are concerned with
treachery and ingratitude. In one, Prince John, by Machiavellian policy, succeeds in arresting the rebels. ' Put not
your trust in princes ' is Mr. Masefield's comment. In the
other, Prince Hal, on coming to the throne, casts off the
aged Falstaff. Many critics have striven to show that
the rejection was necessary, having been foreshadowed in
1 *Henry IV,* and that the audience expected it. But a scene
that needs so much defending must possess some curious
characteristics. From the dramatic point of view, it was

unnecessary to dismiss Falstaff so cruelly, and the scene sends the audience away dissatisfied. But from another point of view, it was necessary for Shakespeare to dismiss Falstaff brutally. Mr. J. A. Fort, in his study of the *Sonnets*, has suggested a reason. Prince Hal's dismissal of Falstaff is a dramatic projection of Southampton's break with Shakespeare. No other explanation squares with the facts. It may be argued that Falstaff represents the limit of the poet's dramatic imagination, and that no progress was possible until Falstaff had been cast off. This is undoubtedly true, but some external stimulus was necessary to make that progress possible.

The theme of ingratitude is of prime importance in *Julius Caesar*. *Et tu Brute* is the keystone of the play. If these words were derived from a source-play, it is significant that Shakespeare did not translate them.

> This was the most vnkindest cut of all.
> For when the Noble *Cæsar* saw him stab,
> Ingratitude, more strong then Traitors armes,
> Quite vanquish'd him : then burst his Mighty heart,
> And in his Mantle, muffling vp his face,
> Euen at the Base of *Pompeyes* Statuë
> (Which all the while ran blood) great *Cæsar* fell.

Another theme, closely allied to ingratitude, is the fickleness of the mob, for which Plutarch provided the material. The two themes are linked in the first scene in the play, where Marullus reproaches the commoners making holiday to see Caesar, and to rejoice in his triumph.

BETRAYAL

Wherefore reioyce ?
What Conquest brings he home ?
What Tributaries follow him to Rome,
To grace in Captiue bonds his Chariot Wheeles ?
You Blockes, you stones, you worse then senslesse things :
O you hard hearts, you cruell men of Rome,
Knew you not *Pompey* ?   Many a time and oft
Haue you climb'd vp to Walles and Battlements,
To Towres and Windowes ?   Yea, to Chimney tops,
Your Infants in your Armes, and there haue sate
The liue-long day, with patient expectation,
To see great *Pompey* passe the streets of Rome :
And when you saw his Chariot but appeare,
Haue you not made an Vniuersall shout,
That Tyber trembled vnderneath her bankes
To heare the replication of your sounds,
Made in her Concaue Shores ?
And do you now put on your best attyre ?
And do you now cull out a Holyday ?
And do you now strew Flowers in his way,
That comes in Triumph ouer *Pompeyes* blood ?
Be gone,
Runne to your houses, fall vpon your knees,
Pray to the Gods to intermit the plague
That needs must light on this Ingratitude.

It may be suggested that Shakespeare's obvious bitterness
was connected with the lynching of Cinna the poet. The
other poet tries to offer advice to Brutus and Cassius, and
he is summarily ejected. (Had Shakespeare endeavoured
to advise his patron or Essex on political matters, and been

149

told to mind his own business ?) Caesar himself faints at the filthy smell of the mob.

Another recurrent and associated theme is the hatred of flatterers, which we noticed in our discussion of *Richard II*. Decius describes how Caesar

> Loues to heare,
> That Vnicornes may be betray'd with Trees,
> And Beares with Glasses, Elephants with Holes,
> Lyons with Toyles, and men with Flatterers,
> But, when I tell him, he hates Flatterers,
> He sayes, he does ; being then most flattered.

Caesar, himself, reproves Metellus for his base spaniel fawning, and Whiter has shown how intimately dogs and flatterers were associated in Shakespeare's mind. Antony fears that he may be thought a flatterer for making friends with the conspirators, and the bitterest insult he can offer to Brutus and Cassius is to call them flatterers, a term that does not seem pointedly appropriate to either of them. In the fourth act, Brutus and Cassius quarrel. Cassius says :

> A friendly eye could neuer see such faults,

and Brutus replies :

> A Flatterers would not, though they do appeare
> As huge as high Olympus.

The theme of cooling and cold friendship to which we have already drawn attention in *As You Like It*, recurs in

BETRAYAL

Julius Caesar. Brutus assures Lucillius that the distant manner in which Cassius has received him is a trustworthy omen.

> Thou hast describ'd
> A hot Friend, cooling : Euer note *Lucillius,*
> When Loue begins to sicken and decay
> It vseth an enforced Ceremony.
> There are no trickes, in plaine and simple Faith :
> But hollow men, like Horses hot at hand,
> Make gallant shew, and promise of their Mettle :
> But when they should endure the bloody Spurre,
> They fall their Crests, and like deceitfull Iades
> Sinke in the Triall.

One of the main ideas of the play is finely described by Mr. Masefield :

Shakespeare ' saw old Rome, full of life, strong in its order, moving as though the wars and winter were over, and spring come, with peace . . . He saw life in its essentials for what it was, an order of intense power, revolving with immense energy about a centre or axle, like a spinning-wheel. . . . Any upsetting of that spinning, from whatever motive . . . is devilish and from a hellish source of broken rhythm and disharmony '.

Professor Stoll has shown that Brutus's motives for killing Caesar are left in obscurity, and though the argument has been pursued a little too strenuously, there can be no doubt that Shakespeare might safely have made more of the Republican ideal about which Plutarch has much to say.

L 151

Caesar's ambition is never made apparent, and the fear that he will misuse his power, as Brutus admits, ' will beare no colour '. All he can say is :

It is the bright day, that brings forth the Adder.

In fact, it is clear either that Shakespeare did not believe in the Republican ideal, or, more probably, that he was not concerned with it in this particular play. Our own belief is that, in the character of Brutus, he was investigating the psychology of betrayal, and, since the study was objective, it is unsatisfactory. He could not conceive how Brutus, even at the call of duty, could stab his friend. To him, all betrayal was irrational. There was, however, one side of Brutus's character which was not an enigma :

> Betweene the acting of a dreadfull thing,
> And the first motion, all the *Interim* is
> Like a *Phantasma*, or a hideous Dreame :
> The *Genius*, and the mortall Instruments
> Are then in councell, and the state of a man,
> Like to a little Kingdome, suffers then
> The nature of an Insurrection.

This might well be a commentary on *Hamlet*, and the two plays are intimately connected. The tempest which preceded Caesar's death is recalled in *Hamlet* :

> In the most high and palmy state of Rome,
> A little ere the mightiest *Iulius* fell
> The graues stood tenantlesse, and the sheeted dead
> Did squeake and gibber in the Roman streets.

BETRAYAL

Hamlet, in the graveyard, meditates characteristically how

> Imperious *Cæsar* dead, and turn'd to Clay,
> Might stoppe a hole, to keepe the wind away.
> O that that earth which kept the world in awe,
> Should patch a wall t'expell the winters flaw.

The presence of Caesar in Shakespeare's mind is attested even by Polonius who enacted Julius Caesar at the university.

In the minds both of Brutus and of Hamlet, there is a conflict between intuition and duty. Brutus is deluded by superstition, by the wiles of Cassius and by a perverted sense of duty into the assassination of Caesar. The conflict in the mind of Hamlet needs no underlining. To Mr. Masefield, *Hamlet* represents a questioning of the vision just manifested in *Julius Caesar*, but this seems a misapprehension, and one that he himself scotches in *Shakespeare and the Spiritual Life*. Brutus misinterpreted the supernatural phenomena, which were an attempt to save the life of Caesar, not to urge on his assassination. Shakespeare wished to project into these phenomena his belief in order, and our next task is to examine the significance of ' order ' to his mind.

The study of the ' Ill May-Day ' scene in *Sir Thomas More* has drawn attention to Shakespeare's views on ' order ', especially as expressed in the Cade scenes in *Henry VI* and in *Coriolanus*. There are four associated themes. First, there is the respect for order of any sort, in the state or Nature, for example. The best instance of this is in *Troilus and Cressida*.

THE VOYAGE TO ILLYRIA

The heauens them-selues, the plannets and this center
Obserue degree, prioritie and place,
Insisture, course, proportion, season, forme,
Office, and custome, in all line of order.

Ulysses, in the same speech, laments

This *chaos*, when degree is suffocate.

In *Measure for Measure*, there is a similar idea expressed by
the Duke :

So our Decrees,
Dead to infliction, to themselues are dead,
And libertie, plucks Iustice by the nose ;
The Baby beates the Nurse, and quite athwart
Goes all decorum.

Secondly, Shakespeare equates ' the state of man ' with the
political organization, for example, in *Julius Caesar* :

The state of a man
Like to a little Kingdome, suffers then
The nature of an Insurrection.

One passage has already been quoted in the last chapter
but one :

Let Order die,
And let this world no longer be a stage,
To feed contention in a lingring act :
But let one spirite of the first borne Cain
Raigne in all bosomes.

BETRAYAL

There is a passage also, in *Henry V* to the same effect :

> Therefore doth heauen diuide
> The state of man in diuers functions,
> Setting endeuour in continual motion . . .
> for so worke the Hony Bees,
> Creatures that by a rule in Nature teach
> The Act of Order to a peopled Kingdome.

In Hamlet's address to his mother, the connection is even more clearly apparent :

> Rebellious hell,
> If thou canst mutine in a Matrons bones . . .

Thirdly, Shakespeare equates orderly government and music, and, conversely, rebellion and discord. Ophelia laments Hamlet's madness :

> And I . . .
> Now see that noble and most soueraigne reason
> Like sweet bells iangled out of time, and harsh.

And love, finally, is equated with order, and, conversely, hate with disorder :

> Perdition catch my Soule
> But I do loue thee : and when I loue thee not,
> Chaos is come againe.

These associated ideas are the very basis of Shakespeare's thought for the next ten years, and their occurrence and recurrence is an infallible sign of the close engagement of the poet's personality. They were the stops in the recorder, and the tunes the dramatic actions they inform. We shall have occasion to return to this linked imagery when we come to discuss *Troilus and Cressida* and *King Lear*, but we must turn first to *Hamlet*, to the tragedy that the world has seen fit to value beyond any other, and endeavour to view it in relationship to the scheme we have so far outlined.

The over-reflective intellectualism which Coleridge discerned in Hamlet's character was not so much a questioning of the vision as a fatal ability to see every side of every question.

The result of my personal investigation into the minds of men who have had to face similar situations (writes Dr. Somerville in his stimulating, if wayward book, *Madness in Shakespearian Tragedy*) has not only confirmed my opinion that the condition is one of fear, but has, as it seems to me, thrown a good deal of light on the actual cause of this fear, and led me to the conclusion that in all these cases a very common, subconscious mental process known as identification takes place—that is to say, a process by which one person subconsciously identifies his own personality with that of another. It is a sort of mental projection which accomplishes subconsciously that which is implied in the familiar saying, ' Put yourself in his place.'

Dr. Somerville goes on to show that Shakespeare himself is the best example of one who perfectly identifies himself with his characters, and this suggests a reason for supposing that Hamlet partook largely of the character of Shakespeare, as Keats declared. Dr. Somerville continues :

BETRAYAL

The would-be slayer, before the acting of a dreadful thing, had, in *feeling*, unwittingly changed places with the victim, and in this way, when proceeding to take the life of another, he would be seized by a terrible fear very much akin to that instinctive dread—present in the subconscious of everyone—of passing suddenly into the unknown . . . Hamlet was almost ideally fashioned for the accomplishment of this act of mentally changing places with people. He had the power, and was constantly using it, subconsciously, of intimately associating himself with others. . . . This subtle process of identification is also facilitated by any circumstances that tend to form an associative link between the principals . . . Claudius and Hamlet had this in common, that they both were worshippers at the shrine of the same goddess.

Dr. Somerville concludes his chapter on *Hamlet* by stating that

In his vivid pictures of these opposite emotional states in Hamlet, Shakespeare is probably—nay, almost certainly —giving us a glimpse at a similar duality in his own personality.

The content of much of Hamlet's conversation and of the third soliloquy, in particular, is not essential to the plot. Shakespeare was himself unpacking his heart with words. To Shakespeare, as to Hamlet, the uses of the world were weary, stale, flat and unprofitable, and it seemed to be peopled with drunkards. Something was rotten in the state, the times were out of joint, and Fortune a strumpet. The world was a prison. The firmament seemed only a

foul and pestilent congregation of vapours. He had bad
dreams. Only the fear of them averted his suicide. Life
was one long calamity.

> Th' oppressors wrong, the proude mans contumely,
> The pangs of despiz'd loue, the lawes delay,
> The insolence of office, and the spurnes
> That patient merrit of th' vnworthy takes . . .

Hamlet did not suffer from any of these evils, but Shakespeare certainly did. Men were arrant knaves all, and the
women were hypocritical harlots. Purpose was but the
slave to memory.

> The great man downe, you marke his fauourite flyes . . .
> And hetherto doth loue on fortune tend,
> For who not needes, shall neuer lacke a friend,
> And who in want a hollow friend doth try,
> Directly seasons him his enemy.

Even Claudius is made to say :

> In the corrupted currents of this world,
> Offences guilded hand may showe by iustice,
> And oft tis seene the wicked prize it selfe
> Buyes out the lawe.

The rose is taken off from the fair forehead of innocent
love, and a blister set in its place. Marriage vows are
as false as dicers' oaths. Religion is a rhapsody of
words.

BETRAYAL

For in the fatnesse of these pursie times
Vertue it selfe of vice must pardon beg,
Yea curbe and wooe for leaue to doe him good.

Kings go a progress through the guts of a beggar. The
noble dust of Alexander stops a bung-hole, and Caesar's
dust is used to patch a wall. ' Divine ' ambition leads
men to find quarrel in a straw, to fight for an egg-shell,
for a plot which is not tomb enough to hide the slain.
Horatio's loyal friendship, Hamlet's enthusiasm for the
theatre, and the flights of angels that sing him to his rest
are the only consolations.

We see, therefore, that the problem of delay, about which
the critics have written so voluminously, is an unreal one.
That is not the real point of the play, which is about disillusionment. Furthermore, the problem arose because
Shakespeare imagined himself as the hero of a play which
required only a simple thoughtless soldier ; and because
Shakespeare was giving expression to his own views on the
world, including a discussion of the art of acting and of the
war of the theatres, because he himself had come to no
conclusions on the problem of revenge, we can infer many
reasons why Hamlet did not kill the King. Miss Caroline
Spurgeon has drawn attention to the prevalence of disease-
imagery in the play, and the only legitimate conclusion we
can draw from this is that Shakespeare was disgusted with
life. It may be argued that he was embodying in Hamlet
some of the characteristics of the melancholic man, but the
imagery reveals that it is Shakespeare who is melancholy,
and those who would explain this attitude as the result of
literary fashion or mental climate, have to face the fact, the
undoubted fact, that Shakespeare was himself one of the

creators of that fashion and of that climate. At the present time, Mr. T. S. Eliot and Mr. Aldous Huxley have captured the post-war disillusionment so successfully that it is impossible to avoid the conclusion that they themselves had suffered from it.

The disease-imagery is largely concerned with the pox, and it is fairly evident that the unrest in Shakespeare's mind was connected with sex, and that he expressed his disgust by the use of imagery connected with venereal disease. For the statement of these problems in a more isolated form, we have only to examine *Troilus and Cressida*, written at the same time as *Hamlet*.

Troilus and Cressida is too uncompromising a play ever to be popular, and the language offers serious obstacles to the casual reader, but there have been signs, in the last few years, that critics are beginning to realize its importance. Mr. Charles Williams in *The English Poetic Mind* regards the play as crucial, but he believes the second scene of Act II is a serious discussion by Shakespeare on ' value '. So it is, up to a point, but the sting is in the tail. Hector proves conclusively that the Trojans have no justice on their side, and that they ought to let Helen go. But, at the end, he changes his mind.

> *Hectors* opinion
> Is this in way of truth : yet nere the lesse,
> My spritely brethren, I propend to you
> In resolution to keepe *Helen* still,
> For 'tis a cause that hath no meane dependance,
> Vpon our ioynt and seuerall dignities.

Shakespeare is showing how little our actions are guided

by reason ; satirizing the motives men have for going to war.
The bitter portraits of the beefy, brainless Greeks, Ajax and
Achilles, are the portraits of Henry V through Hamlet's
eyes. Both of them are eaten up with conceit, while
Achilles sulks in his tent, partly for love of his ' brach ', his
' male varlet ' Patroclus, partly for a treacherous promise
he has made to Hecuba, and mostly because he hates to serve
under Agamemnon. If, as Professor Dover Wilson thinks,
Shakespeare's Achilles is a portrait of Essex, it is bitter satire
rather than advice that he is offering.

The great speech of Ulysses in Act I, scene iii, ascribes
the failure of the Greeks to the 'neglection of degree'.

> The generalls disdaind
> By him one step below, he by the next,
> That next by him beneath.

Shakespeare may be warning Essex, as Professor Dover
Wilson thinks, against rebellion, or he may be commenting
on its failure.

> Horrors
> Diuert and crack, rend and deracinate,
> The vnitie and married calme of states
> Quite from their fixure.

But there is more in the speech than topical allusion. When
Troilus discovers Cressida's unfaithfulness, his whole
belief in order is overthrown ; and by ' order ' in this
context, Shakespeare, as we have already seen, means the
divine order of the Universe.

THE VOYAGE TO ILLYRIA

If beauty haue a soule this is not shee :
If soules guide vowes, if vowes be sanctimonies,
If sanctimony be the gods delight :
If there be rule in vnitie it selfe,
This was not shee . . .
By-fould authority : where reason can reuolt
Without perdition, and losse assume all reason,
Without reuolt. This is and is not *Cresseid* . . .
The bonds of heauen are slipt, dissolu'd and loosd,
And with another knot fiue finger tied . . .
The fragments, scraps, the bitts and greazie reliques,
Of her ore-eaten faith, are giuen to *Diomed*.

It has been asserted that the attitude of Shakespeare to the Trojan War was that of the Middle Ages, and that the tone of disillusionment came naturally to him as the accepted view of the sixteenth century. If we compare Shakespeare's previous utterances, and they are numerous, it is obvious that the tale of Troy once held for him the most glamorous romantic associations. The tone of disillusionment is his own, and the reason for it is everywhere patent, from the bawdy leers of Pandarus to the railing of Thersites :

Now the rotten diseases of the south, the guts griping ruptures : loades a grauell in the back, lethergies, could palsies, rawe eies, durt rotten liuers, whissing lungs, bladders full of impostume. Sciaticaes lime-kills ith' palme, incurable bone-ach, and the riueled fee simple of the tetter, take and take againe such preposterous discoueries.

Troilus pleads passionately, 'Thinke we had mothers'; he declares :

BETRAYAL

> I am as true as truths simplicity,
> And simpler then the infancy of truth,

and his love is trampled in the mud. It would be less terrible if Cressida were a natural harlot. She is only frail, and Shakespeare seems to be saying : ' Frailty, thy name is woman.' Whatever the cause, there can be no doubt that the sex-nausea is the poet's own. Whether he had suffered a second betrayal, this time by a woman, or whether it is the old feeling of *Sonnet* 20 revived in an acute form by the break with Southampton, we cannot be certain. An interesting pointer to a solution is afforded by the connection between ' rebellion ' and ' flesh ' in the plays. The idea that ' the flesh lusteth against the spirit ' is first contained in a speech in 2 *Henry IV* when Falstaff remarks :

> His grace saies that which his flesh rebels against.

This, however, and Caesar's denial that he

> beares such Rebell blood
> That will be thaw'd from the true quality
> With that which melteth Fooles

are not so heavily charged with the notion of all that ' flesh ' implies as are the subsequent ones. In *All's Well that Ends Well* there are, significantly, two passages. The Countess pleads for Bertram :

> And I beseech your Maiestie to make it
> Naturall rebellion, done i'th blade of youth,

163

THE VOYAGE TO ILLYRIA

and this may be compared with Laertes' advice to Ophelia :

> And in the morne and liquid dewe of youth
> Contagious blastments are most iminent,
> Be wary then, best safety lies in feare,
> Youth to it selfe rebels, though none els neare.

The words of Polonius in the same scene echo the thought :

> These blazes daughter
> Giuing more light then heate, extinct in both.

Othello, taking the hand of Desdemona, tells her there is

> A yong, and sweating Diuell heere
> That commonly rebels.

Kent upbraids the flatterers who

> smooth euery passion
> That in the natures of their Lords rebell,

and Octavius complains of Antony's neglect of duty :

> 'Tis to be chid :
> As we rate Boyes, who being mature in knowledge,
> Pawne their experience to their present pleasure,
> And so rebel to iudgement.

Troilus laments that :

> sometimes we are diuells to our selues :
> When we will tempt the frailty of our powers,

but the most significant of such passages comes from the obviously late *Sonnet* 146 :

> Poore soule the center of my sinfull earth,
> Feeding these rebbell powres that thee array.

From the chronology of these passages, we may infer that, by 1600, the stirrings of the flesh were growing more and more distressing, and the simplest hypothesis is to posit a delayed reaction to the betrayal. Shakespeare had overcome the first bitterness, but the break with South-ampton had obliged him to review his attitude to love. He still cherished the illusion that women were inconstant and impure, and, with the increasing desire to find an object for his *affections*, the struggle was correspondingly bitter.

We have already pointed out the significance of ' order ', and the passages we have just cited confirm the association with the idea of ' sex ' which we observed in *Troilus and Cressida*. Much of the imagery in *Hamlet* and in *Troilus and Cressida* is connected with disease, and most of the imagery in *Troilus* and much in *Hamlet* is connected with food. The two sets are associated in various ways. Glut-tony leads to disease, and sexual indulgence is liable to carry with it the penalty of the pox. Thus, gluttony and sex are connected. Furthermore, these are related with the theme of ' order '. In *Coriolanus*, for instance, there is the parable of the members of the body, which relates their functioning to the working of the state :

> I may make the belly Smile,
> As well as speake, it tauntingly replyed

THE VOYAGE TO ILLYRIA

To, th' discontented Members, the mutinous parts
That enuied his receite : euen so most fitly,
As you maligne our Senators, for that
They are not such as you.

Miss Caroline Spurgeon has demonstrated how this allegory is echoed throughout the play by means of the imagery. Coriolanus, for example, is described as a diseased limb. Gluttony upsets the healthy functioning of the body, and so disease is connected with rebellion.

The relation between ' flesh ' and ' spirit ' and the complex of imagery outlined above, will serve to show how intimately in Shakespeare's mind the themes of ' sex ', ' faithlessness ', ' rebellion', ' disease ', and ' gluttony ' were linked. We can see, too, the true significance of his belief in ' order', that it was a reflection of his belief that the flesh should be held in subjection by the spirit, and we may be forgiven if we say here that the insurrection of Caliban is a symbol of the rebellion of the flesh against the spirit, and its failure, of the ultimate victory of the spirit. These considerations, individually and cumulatively, prove, beyond any possibility of contradiction, that the tragic period was provoked by an upheaval connected with sex.

The friendship of Hamlet and Horatio was a statement of what might have been. There is a striking resemblance between the portrait in the *Sonnets* of the men who

haue powre to hurt, and will doe none,
That doe not do the thing, they most do showe,
Who mouing others, are themselues as stone,
Vnmooued, could, and to temptation slow :
They rightly do inherrit heauens graces,

and the speech of Hamlet expressing the same thought :

> Giue me that man
> That is not passions slaue, and I will weare him
> In my harts core, I in my hart of harts
> As I doe thee,

and Hamlet's treatment of Ophelia contrasts with his affection for Horatio.   Some critics have inferred from the continued warnings of Ophelia's relatives on the subject of chastity, from her bawdy song, and from Hamlet's treatment of her, that he had seduced her.   But if Shakespeare had wished the audience to understand that, he would have made it plain.   Possibly this was the case in the *Ur-Hamlet*, but as we have not been favoured with the intimate knowledge of its contents afforded to some critics, we cannot be sure.   In any event, Hamlet's behaviour towards Ophelia can most rationally be explained as a result of the disgust with womankind which took its origin in his mother's remarriage.

One other point calls for comment in *Hamlet*.   John Shakespeare died in 1601, and it seems natural that the character of the dead King should owe something to Shakespeare's recollection of his own father's character.   The event must, at least, have reinforced the poet's meditations on death, and, in the group of plays that we have been discussing, there is clear evidence of a steadily increasing acceptance of death.   Though Plutarch and Montaigne may have taught him much, their philosophy would have been of no interest to Shakespeare, unless he had been prepared by his own development to receive it, and it will be convenient to collect here, from the plays we have been reviewing, some of the more striking passages relating to death. They exhibit, as might be expected, a greater maturity than was evident in the earlier plays.

Already in *Henry IV*, two characters had spoken in scriptural phrase of ' owing God a death ', and Caesar asks :

> What can be auoyded
> Whose end is purpos'd by the mighty Gods ?

And again :

> Cowards dye many times before their deaths,
> The valiant neuer taste of death but once :
> Of all the Wonders that I yet haue heard,
> It seemes to me most strange that men should feare,
> Seeing that death, a necessary end
> Will come, when it will come.

Cassius has a similar thought :

> He that cuts off twenty yeares of life,
> Cuts off so many yeares of fearing death,

and Brutus, speaking of the battle of Philippi, has some words that look forward to *Hamlet* :

> O that a man might know
> The end of this dayes businesse, ere it come :
> But it sufficeth, that the day will end,
> And then the end is knowne.

Hamlet tells Horatio :

BETRAYAL

Not a whit, we defie augury, there is speciall prouidence in the fall of a Sparrowe, if it be now, tis not to come, if it be not to come, it will be now, if it be not now, yet it well come, the readines is all, since no man of ought he leaues, knowes what ist to leaue betimes, let be.

Brutus greets his death stoically :

Night hangs vpon mine eyes, my Bones would rest,
That haue but labour'd, to attaine this houre,

and it is noteworthy that both Brutus and Cassius commit suicide after first discussing it. They play the Roman fool. They have Hamlet's desire

            To die to sleepe
No more, and by a sleepe, to say we end
The hart-ake, and the thousand naturall shocks
That flesh is heire to ; tis a consumation
Deuoutly to be wisht to die to sleepe.

Death to Hamlet is felicity, from which he begs Horatio to absent himself awhile. The rest is silence.

Measure for Measure, though ostensibly a comedy, is crammed with thoughts of death. There is the gloriously disreputable Barnardine who will not consent to be hanged.

I sweare I will not die to day for anie mans perswasion.

There is Claudio, with his terrible fear :

THE VOYAGE TO ILLYRIA

I, but to die, and go we know not where,
To lie in cold obstruction, and to rot,
This sensible warme motion, to become
A kneaded clod ; And the delighted spirit
To bath in fierie floods, or to recide
In thrilling Region of thicke-ribbed Ice,
To be imprison'd in the viewlesse windes
And blowne with restlesse violence round about
The pendant world : or to be worse then worst
Of those, that lawlesse and incertaine thought,
Imagine howling, 'tis too horrible.
The weariest, and most loathed worldly life
That Age, Ache, periury, and imprisonment
Can lay on nature, is a Paradise
To what we feare of death.

This speech is the more impressive because it follows the
superb one by the Duke, which, though perhaps it owes
something to Montaigne, yet seems to express Shakespeare's
own opinion.

Be absolute for death : either death or life
Shall thereby be the sweeter.   Reason thus with life :
If I do loose thee, I do loose a thing
That none but fooles would keepe : a breath thou art,
Seruile to all the skyie-influences,
That dost this habitation where thou keepst
Hourely afflict : Meerely, thou art deaths foole . . .
                        Thou hast nor youth, nor age
But as it were an after-dinners sleep
Dreaming on both.

170

Finally, we may quote the conclusion of *Sonnet* 146, which expresses with a grave and beautiful serenity the Christian attitude to death.

> Then soule liue thou vpon thy seruants losse,
> And let that pine to aggrauat thy store ;
> Buy tearmes diuine in selling houres of drosse :
> Within be fed, without be rich no more,
>   So shalt thou feed on death, that feeds on men,
>   And death once dead, ther's no more dying then.

The Duke's speech to Claudio is the real statement of the problem. ' Be absolute for death.' Shakespeare was vacillating in his own attitude, and the restlessness was painful. Death was felicity, but it was terrible ; and this was the contradiction that Claudio was called on to resolve. He replies :

> To sue to liue, I finde I seeke to die,
> And seeking death, finde life : Let it come on.

He was finding an acceptable attitude to death.

A problem that finds its fullest exposition in Shakespeare in this play is that of chastity. As we can see from its title, *Measure for Measure*, like *Hamlet*, began as a revenge-play. ' With what measure ye mete, it shall be measured to you again.' The imagery, with its frequent weighing metaphors, proves this conclusively, and the Duke, in Act V, declares that the mercy of the law cries out : ' An Angelo for Claudio.' There is much discussion of justice and authority, reward and punishment, and Isabella invokes mercy in the accents of Portia, but in the end it is only the luckless Lucio, the tale-bearer, informer and scandalmonger, who suffers for his misdeeds. The issue has been evaded on almost every level.

The specific problem, then, has been shifted from one of justice to one of chastity. Shakespeare, as we have seen, viewed the body as a microcosm, a little state, in which the baser instincts were liable to rebel against the higher nature of man, and for *Measure for Measure* he took a plot which equated rebellion of the flesh with treason against the state. An old statute awarding death as the penalty for fornication has been revived in Vienna, and Angelo is appointed by the Duke to enforce the operation of the law. Claudio, who has got his betrothed with child 'on a just contract', must suffer death for this. (It is a gross error to imagine that such a sentence was illegal under the provisions of the statute. If this were the case, the play would have no point at all.) The conclusion of the characters is that the statute can never be enforced. Pompey assures Escalus :

If this law hold in *Vienna* ten yeare, ile rent the fairest house in it after three pence a Bay : if you liue to see this come to passe, say *Pompey* told you so,

and he asks :

Do's your Worship meane to geld and splay all the youth of the City ?

In the next scene, the Provost confesses :

All Sects, all Ages smack of this vice.

Isabella asks :

BETRAYAL

Who is it that hath di'd for this offence ?
There's many haue committed it.

Lucio declares :

The vice is of a great kindred ; it is vvell allied, but it is
impossible to extirpe it quite, Frier, till eating and drinking
be put downe ... Why, what a ruthless thing is this
in him, for the rebellion of a Cod-peece, to take away the
life of a man ?

Even Angelo, ' whose blood is very snow-broth' admits
to Isabella that ' we are all fraile'. He proves this when,
desiring Isabella, he makes her virtue the price of her
brother Claudio's reprieve.

This plot, it will be remembered, was not of Shakespeare's devising. It came from Whetstone's play *Promos
and Cassandra*, but, in adapting it to his own use, Shakespeare did strange things to it. In the original play,
Cassandra [Isabella] (we quote from the prose abstract
prefixed to the play)

wonne with the importunitye of hir brother (pleading for
life :) vpon these conditions, she agreede to *Promos* [Angelo].
First that he should pardon her brother, and after marry
her. *Promos* as feareles in promisse, as carelesse in performance, with sollemne vowe, sygned her conditions : but
worse then any Infydel, his will satisfyed, he performed
neither the one nor the other.

The plot subsequently follows almost the same course as
that of *Measure for Measure*, till Cassandra

173

concluded, to make her fortunes knowne vnto the kinge. She (executinge this resolution) was so highly fauoured of the King, that forthwith he hasted to do Iustice on *Promos* : whose iudgement was, to marrye *Cassandra*, to repaire her crased Honour : which donne, for his hainous offence he should lose his head. This maryage solempnised, *Cassandra* tyed in the greatest bondes of affection to her husband, became an earnest suter for his life.

Finally, Cassandra's brother, who has escaped in disguise,

sorrowing the griefe of his sister, bewrayde his safetye, and craued pardon. The Kinge, to renowne the vertues of *Cassandra*, pardoned both him and *Promos*.

Mathematical improbability seldom influenced Shake-speare in his use of plots, but the spectacle of Isabella marrying Angelo after he had betrayed her was too much for his sense of values. The real issue is burked through the substitution of Mariana for Isabella as Angelo's bed-mate and subsequent bride. The same device had been employed by Shakespeare in *All's Well That Ends Well*, and from such a strange piece of dovetailing we can infer that Isabella's purity was a crucial thing that he was unwilling to surrender. Apart from this, all that we can infer is, what was evident from the start, that you cannot reform morals by Act of Parliament. The play could have been successful only if it had developed as a tragedy in which Isabella lost either her virtue or her life, but the plot gave no opportunity for Isabella's death, and, as we have already hinted in Chapter II, if she had surrendered up her purity, then she would not have conformed to the strict pattern of Shakespeare's tragic heroines.

Othello was probably begun in 1604, soon after *Measure for Measure.* We shall best determine its theme by a consideration of the characters of Iago and Othello. Iago has many affinities with Hamlet. Both suffer from an over-reflective intellectualism, but while in Hamlet this paralyzes his power of action, in Iago it spurs him on to act, so that he can feel the power and use the power which the intellect provides. In Hamlet, the intellectualism is harnessed to a tender conscience. In Iago, it is divorced from conscience, and yoked to a motiveless malignity.

Both Hamlet and Iago are destroyed (for it must be remembered that *Othello* is also Iago's tragedy), and Iago's evil nature is not more fatal than Hamlet's exquisite sensibility. The very power of their intellects brings about their ruin. Hamlet's belief in love and goodness is undermined by the conduct of his mother, but it was because he passionately believed in love that he found Gertrude and Ophelia so far from his ideal. Iago's belief in love is not shaken, for it is impossible to conceive that he ever had any. Like Hamlet, he set his intellect to work on it, and he came to the conclusion that it was ' meerly a Lust of the blood, and a permission of the will '. It is a superb stroke of irony that Iago should not believe in love, when the mutual love of Othello and Desdemona is before his eyes, and that his own downfall should be brought about by his wife's love for her mistress. Othello represents that side of Shakespeare's nature which loves. Iago represents the sneering intellect that comments on the love.

What we have said on p. 34 is here relevant. The great writer is the only true psychologist. The clinical psycho-

175

logist collects data about human behaviour, analyses, classifies. The very act of classification falsifies the evidence, because the whole of a character is greater than the sum of the parts, the emotions, instincts, sentiments, desires or complexes into which the psychologist analyses it. As Blake said in *Jerusalem* :

You accumulate Particulars and murder by analysing.

The poet-dramatist does not fall into this error. He exhibits character, not distorted to fit into a scheme or card-index, but as it is, stripped of irrelevancies. To exhibit character is to reveal it. The poet, therefore, is a psychologist whose laboratory is the world. He proceeds by intuition, by imagination, by subconscious understanding. Like Iago, he

knowes all Qualities with a learn'd Spirit
Of humane dealings,

and for this very reason, he must resemble Iago, not in evil, but in that intellectual aloofness, in that horrible probing into motives and possibilities, in that delight in the wielding of intellectual power, and in that inhuman gloating over the mental agony of a fellow-creature :

Looke where he comes : Not Poppy, nor Mandragora,
Nor all the drowsie Syrrups of the world
Shall euer medicine thee to that sweete sleepe
Which thou owd'st yesterday.

This characteristic of Iago, which may be paralleled in

BETRAYAL

Hamlet's treatment of Ophelia, is a magnified representation of one side of Shakespeare's nature. In order to understand human suffering, the poet must experience it in
himself and in others. From the *Sonnets*, it seems, at times,
as if Shakespeare took a wilful delight in the contemplation
of his own suffering. Wordsworth reproved the philosopher who would peep and botanize upon his mother's
grave, but that, as the precision of Wordsworth's denial
would imply, is a symbolic statement of what the poet must
do. As Keats wrote :

The poetical character ' has as much delight in con-
ceiving an Iago as an Imogen. What shocks the virtuous
philosopher delights the chameleon poet . . . A poet is
the most unpoetical of anything in existence, because he
has no Identity—he is continually informing and filling
some other body.'

Coleridge realized that *Othello* was not primarily a
tragedy of jealousy. The tragedy lies in the fact that the
hero is deceived by a man cleverer than himself into believing
Desdemona false. The main theme of the play is not
jealousy, but the shattering of faith. It is true that Shakespeare has incorporated in the character of Othello the
traits of a jealous man as depicted in the psychological
text-books of the time. It is true that Othello is jealous ;
but it is a very peculiar species of jealousy, one that springs
from the shattering of an ideal of love and purity.

If she be false . . . Heauen mocks it selfe.

In Desdemona are incarnated the ideals of truth and
beauty, and Othello loves her with all his soul.

THE VOYAGE TO ILLYRIA

Perdition catch my Soule
But I do loue thee : and when I loue thee not,
Chaos is come againe.

Othello allows his faith in Desdemona, his faith in truth
and beauty and love, to be shaken, to be undermined, almost
to be destroyed, because he accepts what the intellect puts
forward as a proof. He believes Iago, he allows his
natural intuitive faith to be destroyed by a mere intellectual
proof, and that is his tragedy. In a sense, it was Shakespeare's too. That he really had been betrayed is immaterial to the argument. The point is, that he generalized
from a particular instance, and so lost his faith in love and
virtue, this, moreover, in spite of the vision of the Phoenix,
in which he had reasserted his faith after the betrayal.

It may be argued that Shakespeare never lost his belief
in love and virtue and faithfulness, because Desdemona and
Cordelia were 'faithful unto death'. But the phrase is
pointedly appropriate. The corollary of Shakespeare's
belief in the frailty of women was the necessity of destroying the exceptions. Desdemona and Cordelia are innocent
and beautiful and true. For that very reason they must
die. There is a passage in *Othello* that has puzzled the
commentators. In the last scene, Desdemona protests
that her sins are loves she bears to Othello. His reply is a
strange one :

I, and for that thou dy'st.

The words are pregnant with meaning. Shakespeare,
after *The Phoenix and the Turtle*, never lost his belief in
beauty, truth and goodness, but during the tragic period

he could not believe that they were incarnated in living women.

We have touched on so many subjects in this chapter that the reader may find it useful if we recapitulate its main argument. In 1598 Shakespeare was betrayed by Southampton, who possibly may have let it be understood that Shakespeare had resigned the Dark Lady for money, and this betrayal, accompanied by dreams, omens, and premonitions of death, was the dynamic cause of the tragic period. His friendship with Southampton had collapsed, and he was unable or unwilling to lavish on a woman the affection he had reserved for him. The isolation grew stronger as time passed, and, ironically enough, it was combined with that external sociability which impressed his fellows. The break with Southampton did not release him from his bonds. Most probably it resulted in an attempt to bury his bitter memories in sexual indulgence. The main themes of his plays, therefore, at the turn of the century, were the thoughts of this betrayal, the disillusionment which sprang from it, and a refusal to submit wholeheartedly to love for a woman.

NOTE. Generations of critics have ransacked the dictionary to find words of praise for Shakespeare's heroines. Shelley is typical of them all :

> A wonder of this earth,
> Where there is little of transcendent worth—
> Like one of Shakespeare's women.

Except for traces of the Dark Lady in the early heroines, and except for the obvious vitality of the bawds and the whores, there is little in Shakespeare's women to indicate that they were real before Cleopatra. Rosalind, Viola, and Portia are magnificent, but they are not human. They are portraits of Shakespeare's ideal, but there is no evidence to show that either it or they existed in the flesh. Even Dorothy Osborne is a poor substitute for Rosalind. The reason, of course, is that the heroines were not drawn from life, but from an idealization of Southampton.

The emancipation of women in the past few generations has made possible the realization of Shakespeare's dreams. The heroines of modern novels, when they are not intolerable, seem based on Shakespeare's ; and since most of the novelists are photographic in their methods, it seems probable that Shakespeare's dreams have come true. One might even trace the modern fashion of short hair to the habit of Shakespeare's heroines who masquerade as boys.

We do not, of course, suggest that women have consciously copied the heroines of the plays ; but men's ideals are largely conditioned by the poetry they read, and the pictures they see, and women have always done their best to understudy the ideals of men. The psychologists assure us that character is made by a process of fiction. We set up an ideal of what we would like to be ; we delude ourselves into the belief that we are like the ideal ; finally the illusion becomes reality. This process is set forth allegorically in Max Beerbohm's *The Happy Hypocrite*.

Put briefly, Shakespeare's plays contain not only an idealized portrait of the English character in the age of Elizabeth, but a prophetic portrait of the English character as it has since developed. ' Poets are the hierophants of an unapprehended aspiration.'

VII

INFERNO

' He descended into Hell.'

VII

ONE of the most striking characteristics of *Julius Caesar* was the use to which Shakespeare put omens and portents :

> In the most high and palmy state of Rome,
> A little ere the mightiest *Iulius* fell
> The graues stood tenantlesse, and the sheeted dead
> Did squeake and gibber in the Roman streets ;
> And euen the like precurse of fearce euents,
> As harbindgers preceading still the fates
> And prologue to the *Omen* comming on
> Haue heauen and earth together demonstrated
> Vnto our Climatures and countrymen ;
> As starres with traines of fier, and dewes of blood
> Disasters in the sunne ; and the moist starre,
> Vpon whose influence *Neptunes* Empier stands,
> Was sicke almost to doomesday with eclipse.

We are made to feel that the whole order of the universe is being overthrown by the assassination of Caesar. Similarly, the murder of Duncan is so appalling that ' it raises a storm in the spiritual world '. Lamentings are heard in the air, and prophesying with accents terrible of dire combustion and confused events. In the same way, the casting-out of Lear by his daughters brings on, not only the madness of the King, but the madness of the elements as well :

THE VOYAGE TO ILLYRIA

The tempest in my mind,
Doth from my sences take all feeling else,
Saue what beates there, Filiall ingratitude.

It cannot be doubted that these storms were used by Shakespeare, probably unconsciously, to bring home to the audience the horror of the deeds of Brutus, of Macbeth, and of Goneril and Regan, deeds which seemed to violate the laws of Nature. On the other hand, the underplot of Gloucester and his sons makes it quite plain that Shakespeare wishes us to understand that the conduct of the evil sisters is by no means unique. It is significant, too, that there are so many references to Nature. Both Lear and Edmund pray to her :

' Thou Nature art my Goddesse,' cries Edmund, ' to thy
        Law
My seruices are bound.'

Lear invokes Nature :

            Deere Goddesse, heare :
    Suspend thy purpose, if thou did'st intend
    To make this Creature fruitfull :
    Into her Wombe conuey stirrility,
    Drie vp in hir the Organs of increase,
    And from her derogate body, neuer spring
    A Babe to honor her.

In his curse of Cordelia, Lear mentions the sun and the stars and Hecate, but no other deity, and later Cordelia is described as redeeming Nature from the general curse.

INFERNO

It may be argued quite plausibly that the setting in a pagan world may be due in part to the censorship, but the references to Nature are so frequent that they cannot be fortuitous. As a contrast to them, there is much use of the word 'unnatural'. The King of France doubts whether Cordelia's offence can be 'of such unnatural degree', Gloucester calls Edgar an 'unnatural brutish villain', Edmund pretends that he has read a prophecy about eclipses causing unnaturalness between child and parent, and he later refers to Edgar's 'unnatural purpose'. Lear calls Goneril and Regan 'unnatural hags', and Gloucester describes their behaviour as 'unnatural dealing'. Kent, too, speaks of Lear's 'unnatural sorrow'. It is, indeed, filial ingratitude which is at the root of this unnaturalness.

> Is it not as this mouth should teare this hand
> For lifting food too't ?

In this connexion, the disease imagery is noteworthy :

> But yet thou art my flesh, my blood, my Daughter,
> Or rather a disease that's in my flesh,
> Which I must needs call mine. Thou art a Byle,
> A plague sore, or imbossed Carbuncle,
> In my corrupted bloud.

Ingratitude is so unnatural that it is like a disease, and, by a transference of thought, the ungrateful person becomes the disease.

In the last chapter we showed the personal significance of ingratitude. In *King Lear*, the theme is used with an even greater intensity of meaning. Cressida's unfaithfulness overthrew Troilus's belief in order in the Universe, but not only does Lear's personal tragedy lead to a questioning of the moral government of the Universe, the tempest in his mind is accompanied by a tempest in Nature. The Universe itself is shaken by the ingratitude of Goneril and Regan.

In no other play are there so many references to the gods. No other before it is so rich in metaphysical content. Kent declares :

It is the stars,
The stars aboue vs gouerne our conditions,

and he is supported by Gloucester :

These late Eclipses in the Sun and Moone portend no good to vs : though the wisedome of Nature can reason it thus, and thus, yet Nature finds it selfe scourg'd by the sequent effects. Loue cooles, friendship falls off, Brothers diuide. In Cities, mutinies ; in Countries, discord ; in Pallaces, Treason ; and the Bond crack'd, 'twixt Sonne and father. This villaine of mine comes vnder the prediction ; there's Son against Father, the King fals from byas of Nature, there's Father against Childe. We haue seene the best of our time. Machinations, hollownesse, treacherie, and all ruinous disorders follow vs disquietly to our Graues.

As Mr. Murry has pointed out, it is always the villains who boast that they have free-will, so it is not surprising that Edmund should comment :

This is the excellent foppery of the world, that when we

are sicke in fortune, often the surfets of our own behauiour, we make guilty of our disasters, the Sun, the Moone, and Starres, as if we were villaines on necessitie, Fooles by heauenly compulsion, Knaues, Theeues, and Treachers by Sphericall predominance. Drunkards, Lyars, and Adulterers by an inforc'd obedience of Planatary influence ; and all that we are euill in, by a diuine thrusting on. An admirable euasion of Whore-master-man, to lay his Goatish disposition on the charge of a Starre.

But on his death-bed he agrees with his brother that :

> The Gods are iust, and of our pleasant vices
> Make instruments to plague vs :
> The darke and vitious place where thee he got,
> Cost him his eyes,

and he replies :

> Th'hast spoken right, 'tis true,
> The Wheele is come full circle, I am heere.

A similar sentiment is expressed by Regan :

> The iniuries that they themselues procure,
> Must be their Schoole-masters.

This would seem more to be Shakespeare's own opinion than the understandable pessimism of the blinded Gloucester, who says :

THE VOYAGE TO ILLYRIA

I haue heard more since :
As Flies to wanton Boyes, are we to th' Gods,
They kill vs for their sport.

Later on, when he is awaiting death, he is told by Edgar :

Men must endure
Their going hence, euen as their comming hither,
Ripeness is all.

Gloucester can only assent to this remark, which bears
upon it the maturity of which it speaks. It reads like a
condensation of the Duke's great speech in *Measure for
Measure*, but its actual expression seems to indicate that
Shakespeare is now feeling with his heart what he had
before comprehended with his intellect alone. It represents a completed stage in the development of his attitude
to death.

Gloucester had tried to commit suicide. Over the body
of Lear, who had suffered a deeper agony, Kent cries :

Vex not his ghost, O let him passe, he hates him,
That would vpon the wracke of this tough world
Stretch him out longer.

Kent himself has a premonition of approaching death :

I haue a iourney Sir, shortly to go,
My Master calls me, I must not say no.

In *Macbeth*, both the hero and his wife envy the murdered
Duncan.

INFERNO

'Tis safer, to be that which we destroy,
Then by destruction dwell in doubtfull ioy,

is echoed by the terrible

Better be with the dead,
Whom we, to gayne our peace, haue sent to peace,
Then on the torture of the Minde to lye
In restlesse extasie.
Duncane is in his Graue :
After Lifes fitfull Feuer, he sleepes well,
Treason ha's done his worst : nor Steele, nor Poyson,
Mallice domestique, forraine Leuie, nothing,
Can touch him further.

Life to them both is a tale told by an idiot, full of sound
and fury, signifying nothing. Life to Shakespeare could
never have signified nothing. By reducing its futility to
artistic expression, he transcended it. 'Freedom,' wrote
Hegel, 'is knowledge of necessity.' Timon regards life
as a long sickness, and he looks forward to annihilation :

Nothing brings me all things.

When Shakespeare wrote this, the worst had been said.
  The evil that provoked these thoughts of death is most
penetratingly analysed in *King Lear*. Here, Shakespeare
took upon himself the mystery of the world. Cordelia
is destroyed, as Desdemona and Ophelia had been, because
she is beautiful and constant. In his play *A l'Ombre du Mal*,
Lenormand has expressed a similar idea through the mouth
of Rougé :

THE VOYAGE TO ILLYRIA

To do good is to draw disaster on one's own head . . .
The love of good doesn't always draw the thunderbolt on
oneself, but sometimes on others, on unknown people at
the other side of the globe. . . . The converse is also true.
Hate and cruelty preserve us. Doing harm keeps oneself
from harm. If we are still alive after twenty years of Africa,
twenty years of massacre, plague, and treachery, it is because
we have both lived in the shadow of evil.

But in Shakespeare's plays the villainous are not pre-
served. Their evil destroys themselves no less than the
virtuous, and when he wrote *King Lear*, the poet did not
doubt that it was better to be Cordelia dead in the arms of
her father than to be either of her pelican sisters :

> We are not the first,
> Who with best meaning haue incurr'd the worst :
> For thee oppressed King I am cast downe,
> My selfe could else out-frowne false Fortunes frowne.

Over such sacrifices, indeed, the gods themselves throw
incense.

In *Hamlet*, Shakespeare had complained of the law's
delay, the insolence of office, and the spurns that patient
merit of the unworthy takes. Now, in *King Lear*, he
exhibits, for the first time, a deep sense of social injustice :

> Thorough tatter'd cloathes smal vices do appear :
> Robes, and Furr'd gowns hide all. Plate sinnes with Gold,
> And the strong Lance of Iustice, hurtlesse breakes.

This is Lear, mad. During the tempest, he has an even
greater passage :

INFERNO

Poore naked wretches, where so ere you are
That bide the pelting of this pittilesse storme,
How shall your House-lesse heads, and vnfed sides,
Your lop'd, and window'd raggednesse defend you
From seasons such as these ?   O I haue tane
Too little care of this : Take Physicke, Pompe,
Expose thy selfe to feele what wretches feele,
That thou maist shake the superflux to them,
And shew the Heauens more iust.

The vision of the world's injustice, his understanding that
the great image of authority is a dog obeyed in office, leads
Shakespeare farther on his destined course. All are
equally guilty, and therefore all are equally innocent :

None do's offend, none, I say none.

But Lear was mad when he said this, and his attitude to
Goneril and Regan shows that they, at least, had not
received his forgiveness.   Shakespeare could not accept the
mystery of iniquity yet.

In all the plays of this group, the theme of ingratitude
is apparent.   The filial ingratitude of Lear's daughters, of
Edmund, the treachery of Macbeth to his host, benefactor,
and liege-lord, the hereditary ingratitude of Timon's
friends, the ingratitude of the people of Rome to Coriolanus
—the examples are too frequent to be fortuitous.   To
Shakespeare, the very heart of the mystery was ingratitude.

The corollary of the theme of ingratitude in *King Lear* is
a powerful sex-disgust. Lear was responsible for the
birth of his children, and his grief and madness at their
behaviour is coloured with his attitude to the instinct that

THE VOYAGE TO ILLYRIA

had brought them into the world. But it is to be noted
that the sex-disgust is not confined to the King himself.
Edgar, when he is pretending to be mad, says that he slept
in the contriving of lust, and waked to do it ; the Fool's
bitter jests often have a sexual significance ; Gloucester is
an ' old lecher ' ; and the lasciviousness of the three villains
needs no comment. We have already drawn attention in
our fifth chapter to the hunting theme, and its relation to
the word ' venery ', and we may recall the opening scene of
Twelfth Night. There is no evidence to show that Shakespeare was consciously aware that neurosis and madness
are often caused by a sex-upheaval, and it seems fairly evident, from its ramifications throughout the play, that the
sex-disgust is the poet's own.

   Lear desires to have some civet to cleanse his imagination.
The poet was speaking.

Adultery ?

Thou shalt not dye : dye for Adultery ?   No,
The Wren goes too't, and the small gilded Fly
Do's letcher in my sight.
Let Copulation thriue : for Glousters bastard Son
Was kinder to his Father, then my Daughters
Got 'tweene the lawfull sheets.
Too't Luxury pell-mell, for I lacke Souldiers.
Behold yon simpring Dame,
Whose face betweene her Forkes presages Snow ;
That minces Vertue, & do's shake the head
To heare of pleasures name.
The Fitchew, nor the soyled Horse goes too't
With a more riotous appetite :
Downe from the waste they are Centaures,

192

Though Women all aboue :
But to the Girdle do the Gods inherit,
Beneath is all the Fiends.   There's hell, there's darkenes,
There is the sulphurous pit ; burning, scalding stench,
　　consumption . . .
Thou Rascall Beadle, hold thy bloody hand :
Why dost thou lash that Whore ?   Strip thy owne
　　backe,
Thou hotly lusts to vse her in that kind,
For which thou whip'st her.

　　It is only a step from *King Lear* to the tirades of *Timon*.
Nobody has doubted the authenticity of the most terrible
passages :
　　　　　　To generall Filthes
　　Conuert o' th' Instant greene Virginity,
　　Doo't in your Parents eyes . . .
　　　　　　　Maide, to thy Masters bed,
　　Thy Mistris is o' th' Brothell . . .
　　　　　　　Thou cold Sciatica,
　　Cripple our Senators that their limbes may halt
　　As lamely as their Manners.   Lust, and Libertie
　　Creepe in the Mindes and Marrowes of our youth . . .
　　　　　　　Itches, Blaines,
　　Sowe all th' Athenian bosomes, and their crop
　　Be generall Leprosie : Breath, infect breath,
　　That their Society (as their Friendship) may
　　Be meerely poyson . . .
　　Gold . . .
　　　　　　　This is it
　　That makes the wappen'd Widdow wed againe ;
　　Shee, whom the Spittle-house, and vlcerous sores,

THE VOYAGE TO ILLYRIA

Would cast the gorge at.   This Embalmes and Spices
To' th' Aprill day againe.

Years before, Shakespeare, in the springtime of his love, had
written :

> Thou art thy mothers glasse and she in thee
> Calls backe the louely Aprill of her prime.

From his love he had been absent in the spring,

> When proud pide Aprill (drest in all his trim)
> Hath put a spirit of youth in euery thing.

Three years after he had first met Southampton he had
written again :

> Three Aprill perfumes in three hot Iunes burn'd
> Since first I saw you fresh,

and in *The Two Gentlemen of Verona* it is love itself that
is like April :

> Oh, how this spring of loue resembleth
> The vncertaine glory of an Aprill day.

' April ' was a word once consecrated to love in Shakespeare's mind.   Now it is deliberately rubbed in the mire.
Instead of the spring and love, we have lust and its
concomitant diseases :

> Cracke the Lawyers voyce,
> That he may neuer more false Title pleade,

194

Nor sound his Quillets shrilly : Hoare the Flamen,
That scolds against the quality of flesh,
And not beleeues himselfe.   Downe with the Nose,
Downe with it flat, take the Bridge quite away . . .
                    Plague all,
That your Actiuity may defeate and quell
The sourse of all Erection.

The reader can be left in no doubt that Shakespeare himself was disgusted with sex and everything connected with
it.   All women seemed to be whores, except the imaginary
Cordelia, who was too good to live.   Love was only a
lust of the blood, and its natural and inevitable sequence
the pox.   This is not the gentle Shakespeare of the Edward-
ian biographer.   It is a man tortured by his own thoughts,
disgusted by his feelings, hating his fellow men.   It is a
man bound on a wheel of fire, a man to whom life was
a nightmare, a man who, when he thought it, if not when
he wrote it, was on the last verge of sanity, a man who was
saved only by his sense of humour, and by the detachment
which that implies.

Even in *Macbeth*, which preceded *Timon of Athens*, though
the theme might seem to forbid it, sex is by no means
absent.   The first vice of which Malcolm accuses himself,
in the third scene of Act IV, is lust :

Your Wiues, your Daughters,
Your Matrons, and your Maides, could not fill vp
The Cesterne of my Lust,

and, in his reply, Macduff uses the significant word
' dedicate ' :

195

THE VOYAGE TO ILLYRIA

There cannot be
That Vulture in you, to deuoure so many
As will to Greatnesse dedicate themselues,
Finding it so inclinde.

Macbeth goes to the murder of Duncan with Tarquin's ravishing strides, and, as Whiter pointed out in 1794, there are many echoes of the imagery of *Lucrece*, which serve to indicate (though Whiter did not make this inference) that the theme of *Macbeth* is sexual in origin, and that Shakespeare, ostensibly writing about murder, is, on another level, writing on the theme of lust.[1] This obsession with sex may very well have been caused simply by the break with Southampton, but it seems very probable that Shakespeare had sought oblivion in equivocation with lechery.

From the dress-imagery of *Macbeth*, Miss Spurgeon infers that Shakespeare conceived the protagonist as an insignificant man in a position too big for him, but this conflicts so violently with the conscious meaning of the play that the deduction would be illegitimate unless no other explanation were possible, and this is manifestly not the case. The imagery might indicate that Macbeth was conceived as a square peg in a round hole, an ordinary formula for tragedy. It might be a variation of the theme of injustice so fully exposed in *King Lear* :

Thorough tatterd cloathes smal Vices do appeare :
Robes and Furr'd gownes hide all.

But, on the other hand, it must be connected with the imagery of one of the key-speeches of the play, where life

[1] Murther's as neere to Lust, as Flame to Smoake.—*Pericles* I, i, 138.

is compared to a poor player, and this is the most plausible, for, as Whiter pointed out, both *Macbeth* and *Lucrece* have a considerable amount of imagery derived from the stage.

Mr. L. C. Knights in his interesting essay, *How many children had Lady Macbeth?* vindicates the relevance of certain passages whose point other critics have missed. The famous passage about the different kinds of dogs is an indication that Shakespeare conceived Macbeth's crime as an overthrowing of natural order. Even the prattle of Macduff's son is of importance, and the long dialogue between Malcolm and Macduff, in which the former accuses himself of every conceivable crime, is intended to reflect on Macbeth. And the passage about the King's Evil, which is usually taken as an intrusive compliment to James I, knits up perfectly with the disease-imagery of the last act. The evil from which Scotland suffers is Macbeth himself:

> If thou could'st Doctor, cast
> The Water of my Land, finde her Disease,
> And purge it to a sound and pristine Health,
> I would applaud thee to the very Eccho,
> That should applaude againe.

Another critic, Mgr. Kolbe, has shown that in *Macbeth* the word 'blood' occurs more than a hundred times, 'sleep' and 'night' more than seventy times each:

It cannot now be doubted that he meant to give the whole play the colour of the crime. Duncan's *blood* was shed during his *sleep* in the middle of the *night*. The first of these ideas gave the guilt : the second began the Nemesis or retribution : the third was a parable of the condition of all sin.

There are over a hundred repetitions of the idea of 'confusion', and Mgr. Kolbe believes that Shakespeare deliberately inserted them to emphasize the results of crime, and that there is a 'symmetrical array of all the forces of Evil on the one side and of Good on the other'. It would seem rather to be a case of what Professor Wilson Knight has called 'clustered imagery'. The poet did not apply this 'colouring' deliberately. He conceived the subject so intensely that his language was naturally steeped in the colours of his imagination. *Macbeth*, despite its truncated form, is one of the most interesting plays, from the point of view of imagery. Not only does it throw considerable light on its author's personality, but we can also appreciate to the full a play where the significance of every line is modulated by the overtones of imagery and meaning. It should be noted, however, that the poet's imagination is a good deal more complex than his critics lead us to believe. Mr. Knights and Mgr. Kolbe scarcely overlap in their interpretations, yet both are perfectly sound as far as they go. Most attempts to discover the theme of a play of Shakespeare fail because they attempt to reduce to a formula the poet's elusive complexity. Some would argue that the multitude and diversity of these interpretations reflect only the personal views of the individual critics, but it reflects the richness of the mines, which the innumerable delvers have failed to exhaust.

The state of the text of *Timon of Athens* has been accounted for in several different ways :

1. That Shakespeare was revising the work of other men.

2. That various dramatists completed an unfinished play by Shakespeare.

3. That Shakespeare's method of working was to write a very hasty rough draft, and then to revise in detail, going first to those passages that interested him most ; that he had revised only part of the play, when, for some reason, he put it aside.

4. That the play was clumsily put together, ' assembled ', from the actors' recollections, and that the MS. of the part of Timon was all they had to go on.

This first explanation is surely incredible, even on the assumption that Shakespeare was prevented from finishing his work of revision. The main design of the play seems to be Shakespeare's, and the source is the same as that of the neighbouring plays, *Coriolanus* and *Antony and Cleopatra*, namely, North's *Plutarch*. The second explanation is as difficult as the first. The incompetence of the revisers would surpass all bounds of probability, and we are thrown back on (3) or (4). The very extraordinary rhymed couplets are most unlikely to be the garbled version of Shakespeare's blank verse, and it is equally unlikely that the editors of the First Folio would have gone to such trouble to resurrect a piece especially for the printer. The disturbances in Act II, scene ii, and the long gap between the approach of the Poet and the Painter and their actual appearance, have been brought forward as evidence for (4), but they are equally valid for (2) or (3). The imagery of some of the supposedly spurious scenes is often Shakespearean, even where the verse is hopelessly bad, and the resemblance of the strange couplets to the style of the first two acts of *Pericles* confirms what Sir Edmund Chambers hazarded—that we have to do with a first draft. The reason for the abandonment of *Timon* seems clear, and our own conjecture, made some years ago, that Shakespeare suffered a nervous breakdown, is made also by Sir Edmund Chambers. There were danger signals in *King Lear*. There the poet reached harbour only by running very close to the wind.

By the actual writing of *King Lear*, Shakespeare recovered a measure of serenity. By forcing his emotion into the mould of the play, he was able to control it. The summer landscapes of the fourth act, after the wintry third, suggest that the countryside in early summer had something to do with his temporary recovery. *Macbeth* is more objective, and the personification of evil in the non-human witches is an indication of this. *Coriolanus*, if it came next, is so objective that it seems as if Shakespeare's feelings were not deeply engaged except with the motive of ingratitude. The portrait of Volumnia, however, has tempted some critics to see in it Shakespeare's tribute to his mother, who died in 1608.

In *King Lear*, the virtuous characters outnumber the villains. Kent, the Fool, Cordelia, Edgar, and the servant who resists the blinding of Gloucester are a proof that Shakespeare, when we take into consideration the tempest in his mind, was able to maintain a remarkable balance. He realized that the betrayal he had suffered had upset his judgment, and he utilized to the full the feelings of disgust and horror to which he was a prey, but, with superb artistry, he subordinated them to a conception of life that was broader. His imagination, as he himself realized, was always ahead of his ordinary feelings. There was a certain time-lag. He had to ' grow into the garments of inspiration ', and, if nothing further had occurred, he might have escaped the deeper Inferno of *Timon of Athens*, but when he wrote this, the poet in him was overwhelmed by what he had previously mastered. He could no longer defy the foul fiend. Everything, even his belief in an imagined goodness, was swept away. Perhaps, as Mr. Murry suggests, the *Sonnets* were betrayed into the hands of a piratical publisher. Whether this were the case, or whether it was by pure mischance, their publication could not fail to revive the bitter feelings which the original betrayal had provoked. But this, and the death of Shakespeare's mother in September 1608, need not necessarily be used as evidence. The poet's progress seems to have been marked by an ever-sharpening note of hysteria.

The main theme of *Timon of Athens* is plainly indicated in the first scene of the play, where the Poet's fable is inserted by Shakespeare expressly for that purpose :

I haue vpon a high and pleasant hill
Feign'd Fortune to be thron'd. The Base o' th' Mount
Is rank'd with all deserts, all kinde of Natures
That labour on the bosome of this Sphere,
To propagate their states : among'st them all,
Whose eyes are on this Soueraigne Lady fixt,
One do I personate of Lord *Timons* frame,
Whom Fortune with her Iuory hand wafts to her,
Whose present grace, to present slaues and seruants
Translates his Riuals . . .
All those which were his Fellowes but of late,

THE VOYAGE TO ILLYRIA

Some better then his valew ; on the moment
Follow his strides, his Lobbies fill with tendance,
Raine Sacrificiall whisperings in his eare,
Make Sacred euen his styrrop, and through him
Drinke the free Ayre . . .
When Fortune in her shift and change of mood
Spurnes downe her late beloued ; all his Dependants
Which labour'd after him to the Mountaines top,
Euen on their knees and hands, let him slip downe,
Not one accompanying his declining foot.

Later in the play, in a passage which may not, however,
be Shakespeare's, the Poet proposes to write :

A Satyre against the softnesse of Prosperity, with a
Discouerie of the infinite Flatteries that follow youth and
opulencie.

If Shakespeare wrote the first scene of Act V, it was
conceived in the bitter mood of self-criticism which
inspired the significant and heartfelt lines in the first scene
of the play :

When we for recompence haue prais'd the vild,
It staines the glory in that happy Verse,
Which aptly sings the good.

The anger against flatterers, apparent in *King Lear*, reaches
its highest point, and there are other passages which glance,
perhaps, at the final act of his affection for Southampton,
and recall the speech of Brutus in *Julius Caesar*.

INFERNO

> To liue
> But in a Dreame of Friendship,
> To haue his pompe, and all what state compounds,
> But onely painted like his varnisht Friends

is a passage, which, however rough, is undoubtedly Shake-speare's. It is preceded by the scene in which Timon's faithful servants bid each other farewell, a scene that contains the lines discussed by Mr. Murry :

> His poore selfe
> A dedicated Beggar to the Ayre,
> With his disease, of all shunn'd pouerty,
> Walkes like contempt alone.

Flaminius says of Lucullus, in lines which strikingly combine disease imagery with the theme of friendship :

> Thou disease of a friend, and not himselfe . . .
> This Slaue,
> Vnto his Honor, has my Lords meate in him :
> Why should it thriue, and turne to Nutriment,
> When he is turn'd to poyson ?
> O may Diseases onely worke vpon't.

Not only are ' friendship ' and ' disease ' combined in the same image, but they are linked with another significant type of Shakespearian image—the image of ' food '.

There is a well-founded tradition that Southampton gave Shakespeare a large sum of money to buy property, though the amount, £1,000, seems to be ten times too great, and the passages we have quoted above lead us to believe that the poet is now accusing himself of having praised Southampton for recompense. He had not done so, we can be sure, and it is impossible that he parted from Southampton *after* the Essex conspiracy had failed. What then is the motive of this false accusation against himself? It is compounded of two feelings. He is pretending that he was a time-server to excuse Southampton's treachery, and, as a piece of defence-mechanism, he is pretending he praised for reward. ' I should not care to admit that the *Sonnets* were written out of affection. Southampton is vile, but it is impossible that I was deceived in him, and I must therefore have praised him solely for reward.' That we are not exaggerating the importance of these lines is shown by the poet's own comment :

A thing slipt idlely from me.
Our Poesie is as a Gum, which ooses
From whence 'tis nourisht : the fire i'th'Flint
Shewes not, till it be strooke : our gentle flame
Prouokes it selfe, and like the currant flyes
Each bound it chafes.

This is Shakespeare's most serious utterance on the nature of poetry, and we must accept it for what it is worth.

Moreover, the general tone of the play gives the reader of even moderate sensibility the feeling of being too tense for sanity, and it provokes the belief that Shakespeare's resistance had reached its limits. The tempest of his soul had brought on shipwreck, and the last stage of the voyage to Illyria all but ended in catastrophe. The last agonies cannot be committed to paper, and the words of Æschylus,

INFERNO

at the end of *Prometheus Vinctus*, provide, perhaps, the
least inadequate comment :

Prom.   The tidings that he brings
come stalely to mine ears. It is no shame
to suffer torture at the hands of foes.
I am resigned. Let the sharp lightning flame
be hurled against me, let the air wax wroth
with thunder and demented winds, and may
the Earth itself, from her profoundest depths,
shiver and tremble, and with yeasty surge
gather the ocean waves upon a heap
to drown the eternal stars—to lift me high
on the stern whirlwind of necessity
and cast me into hell. Yet, for all this,
he shall not bring me death.

Her.   His words are madness.
Do you at least that pity his afflictions
hasten to safety, lest the thunderclap
unsettle your reason.

Chor.   What you urge is vain.
Surely your counsel is intolerable.
Shall I turn coward ? Since this man must suffer
I would suffer with him. For I have learned
to hate a traitor. There's no malady
that I hate more than this.

Her.   Remember, then,
what I foretell ; nor, when you are hunted down
by a relentless doom, blame Fortune for it,
nor say at any time that Zeus hath cast you
to unforeseen affliction. 'Tis you yourselves.
Warned and not secretly, for your foolish choice

THE VOYAGE TO ILLYRIA

in the illimitable net of doom
you will be caught.

Prom.   No more in apprehension,
but in very deed, the Earth's convulsed: the sound
of thunder from the depths reverberates
rolling with terror past me : eye-piercing flames
of lightning flash forth dreadful : whirlwinds roar.
And all the winds rise up in mortal strife,
blast against blast outrageous, while the air
is with the sea confounded.   Such is the work
of tyrannous Zeus to make me fear.   O Mother,
O great Mother !   O air that rollest light
to all, both good and evil, thou behold'st
how unjust are the pains which I endure !

VIII

AFTER THE STORM

O braue new world.

MIRANDA *in* THE TEMPEST

VIII

*A*NTONY AND CLEOPATRA was written either
immediately before or soon after the abortive *Timon
of Athens.* In either case, the difficulties of chronology are
considerable, for a vast amount of work must be crowded
into the years 1605–8. Both Sir Edmund Chambers and
the *New Cambridge* editors believe that *Antony and Cleopatra*
precedes *Timon,* but Bradley drew attention to the striking
affinities between *Timon* and *King Lear.* To the argument
that the Shakespeare who had reached in his attitude to
death the serenity of *Antony and Cleopatra* could not have
written *Timon,* Chambers justly replies that brain-
storms come in waves, and that *Timon* may indicate a
relapse.

If the reader adheres to this view, it need not prejudice
his attitude to the larger issues involved. *Antony and
Cleopatra* represents a positive advance in Shakespeare's
attitude to death, and the breakdown of *Timon* might
well have been due to the feverish activity which the
factors discussed in the previous chapter had set up. Metrically, psychologically, and metaphysically, *Antony and
Cleopatra* is the first play of the last period, whatever its
date. Metrically, it exhibits a new freedom, a certain
royal carelessness, born perhaps of even greater fluency
of inspiration. Psychologically, it reflects, at last, a satis-
factory synthesis of the desires and the affections. Metaphysically, it is a poem of the conquest of death by love.
It is certain that Shakespeare was able to write the play
because he had solved the sex-problem of his own life.

It is no less certain that he could not have done so unless he had met a woman in whom his desire and affection could reunite. It can scarcely have been the Dark Lady : most probably it was not. The question is not important. On the other hand, we have here the only tragedy by Shakespeare in which the heroine is of equal importance to the hero, the only play by him[1] in which a woman's death is the dramatic climax. The whole of the fifth act is devoted to Cleopatra's death, by which she is made worthy of Antony. Her faults are by no means glozed. She is a whore, ' a boggler ever ', a liar and a coward, but the royalty and magnificence of her death atones for all. Antony's spirit enters into her, and she is made one with him. Instead of the unedifying spectacle of Venus wooing an innocent youth, we have personified in the tale of Antony and Cleopatra the classical myth of Mars wooing Venus. With the school of criticism that trades in such expressions as ' gilded harlot ' and ' scarlet woman ' we have no patience. Critics, too, who see in the play a moral tale typifying the fall of an empire, are deplorably astray in their reckoning. Doubtless, this sort of thing might apply to the Cleopatra of the first act, but the strengthening of her resolves, the discarding of feminine coquetry, the general development of her character till it reaches the stature of Antony's, all show the ineptitude of this opinion. Dryden came nearer the truth when he styled his version of the play ' All for Love, or the World Well Lost '. *Antony and Cleopatra* is not a tragedy in the same sense as its predecessors. Cleopatra is heroic in her attitude to death. It is noteworthy that Shakespeare altered his source so as to make her efforts to deceive

[1] Queen Katherine's death-scene in *Henry VIII* is by Fletcher.

Octavius purely selfish.   But it is an error to infer that it
was done in order to blacken Cleopatra's character.   On
the contrary, the tragic effect is enhanced by it.   Her
deception of Octavius (one of Shakespeare's prigs) shows
how fiercely she still clung to the hope of life.   The final
sacrifice is a willing and a laudable one.

> Giue me my Robe, put on my Crowne, I haue
> Immortall longings in me.   Now no more
> The iuyce of Egypts Grape shall moyst this lip.
> Yare, yare, good *Iras* ; quicke : Me thinkes I heare
> *Anthony* call : I see him rowse himselfe
> To praise my Noble Act.   I heare him mock
> The lucke of *Cæsar*, which the Gods giue men
> To excuse their after wrath.   Husband, I come.

Here, indeed, with the utterance of the sacred word ' hus-
band ', Shakespeare signalizes the marriage of true minds.
The constancy and its regal setting are the themes by which
the profound composition advances.   The character of
Enobarbus is in powerful contrast to that of Cleopatra.
What he failed to do for the sake of Friendship, Cleopatra
did for the sake of Love.   If to Shakespeare most friendship
still was mere feigning, no longer was loving mere folly.
We are irresistibly reminded of *The Phoenix and the Turtle*.
Here, truly, was Love's Martyr.   Middle age carried away
by passion is liable to provoke n irth, but there is no middle
age to be inferred from *Antony and Cleopatra*.   There is,
rather, the full maturing of the personality and of the body
that moulds it.   Antony's forgiveness of Enobarbus, based
on an insignificant reference in Plutarch, is a sign that Shakespeare had already realized that ' the rarer Action is In

vertue then in vengeance'. In *The Two Gentlemen of Verona* and in *As You Like It* we have unquestionably the same *motiv*, but in both cases there is an artificiality which defeats the intention behind it, a portrayal more of what the poet thought, than of what he felt should be. With the full realization of the futility of revenge, the ultimate synthesis was at last possible. In the forgiveness of Enobarbus we have the germ of the Romances.

The last three acts of *Pericles*, which are all that can be regarded as Shakespeare's perfected work, have been described as a convalescent play. Whatever the relation between this section and the preceding two acts, there can be no doubt that it is complete in itself. It is attractive to suppose (with Sir Edmund Chambers) that Shakespeare made a recovery at Stratford, and that the character of Cerimon is a tribute to his son-in-law, Dr. John Hall :

> I hold it euer
> Vertue and Cunning, were endowments greater,
> Then Nobleness & Riches ; careless Heyres,
> May the two latter darken and expend ;
> But Immortalitie attendes the former,
> Making a man a god : T'is knowne, I euer
> Haue studied Physicke : through which secret Art,
> By turning ore Authorities, I haue
> Togeather with my practize, made famyliar,
> To me and to my ayde, the blest infusions
> That dwels in Vegetiues, in Mettals, Stones :
> And can speak of the disturbances
> That Nature workes, and of her cures.

Cerimon works with the aid of music, as the doctor in

AFTER THE STORM

King Lear had used it to ' wind up ' the untuned and jarring senses of the king. Marina, too, sings to restore Pericles. Music, as Professor Wilson Knight has amply demonstrated, is an integral part of the plays of the last period, and in all Shakespeare's work music is the antithesis of the tempest themes. In his *Myth and Miracle*, Professor Knight says ' the tempest is percurrent in Shakespeare as a symbol of tragedy ', and we may interpret the use of ' tragedy ' to mean all the negation of order that we have encountered in the plays of the Inferno.

Professor Knight has since exhausted all the ramifications of the ' tempest-music ' antithesis in his study *The Shakespearian Tempest*, and we can do no more than cite, with complete acquiescence, his conclusion :

Metaphors and fancies of one period become expanded to plots, the very stuff of intellectual and poetic vision in another.

He has also called attention to the jewel-imagery of *Pericles* :

' Behold
Her ey-lids, cases to those heauenly iewels
Which *Pericles* hath lost,' cries Cerimon,
' Begin to part their fringes of bright gold,
The Diamonds of a most praysed water
Doth appear to make the world twise rich.'

Marina's eyes are like her mother's, ' as Iewell-like, and caste as richly '. These and similar passages show how high a value Shakespeare set on love. It is the pearl of great

213

price which the base Judean flung away when he betrayed his Master.

One of the weaker scenes comes like an echo from an earlier period. The wicked Dionizza scolds her husband in much the same way that Goneril jeers at Albany. But wickedness is now powerless to overcome love and truth. Marina's chastity preserves her in a brothel which makes no concessions to present-day squeamishness. She even converts the whoremongers, and makes the shameless Boult ashamed. The gods are now merciful, and the love of Pericles and Thaisa, which death could not conquer, itself conquers death.

Pericles is in many respects the ' mouldy tale ' Jonson thought it to be. Even in the last three acts to which we have confined ourselves, some important incidents are related by the moral Gower or are given in dumb-show. It is clear that the first two acts could have been omitted, and the remaining three expanded. Some of the glaring improbabilities could have been excised without difficulty. Thaisa ought surely to have tried to communicate with her husband whom she had no reason to suppose dead. But, in spite of these flaws, the story was one that exactly suited Shakespeare's genius in the latter half of 1608. Whatever the involved textual history of the version that has survived, the last three acts remain a little recognized but indisputable masterpiece.

Shakespeare had passed through the tempest of his soul. Like Lear recovering from his madness to the sound of the voice of his Cordelia, the poet was restored to complete sanity. He had recovered his Thaisa, his belief in love and virtue. Pericles is reunited to his daughter, and he hears the music of the spheres.

AFTER THE STORM

It is possible that one of Shakespeare's daughters nursed him back to health, but even if this were not so, the symbolism of the play is beautifully appropriate, and it reappears in all his subsequent plays. ' Did you not name a tempest a birth and a death ? ' asks Marina, and the birth from the sea, which is repeated with slight variations in *The Winter's Tale* and *The Tempest*, is a perfect symbol. Water has always been a dream-symbol of birth and death. Shakespeare, as will be seen, by a natural combination of these two, makes the sea symbolic of rebirth and immortality. The child, too, is a symbol of immortality, and it seems natural to suppose that the poet was experiencing belatedly the joys of fatherhood. The reunion of Pericles and Marina is the re-discovery of his immortality. It is followed by his recovery of Thaisa, the symbolism here obeying a lovely poetic logic.

The power and beauty of the later part of *Pericles* can be demonstrated by a simple comparison. The sister of Katherine, in *Love's Labour's Lost*, was killed by Cupid :

> He made her melancholie, sad, and heauie,
> And so she died : had she bin Light like you,
> Of such a mery nimble stiring spirit,
> She might a bin a Grandam ere she died.

In *Twelfth Night*, Viola describes her love :

> She neuer told her loue,
> But let concealment like a worme i'th budde
> Feede on her damaske cheeke ; she pin'd in thought,
> And with a greene and yellow mellancholly,
> She sate like Patience on a Monument,
> Smiling at greefe.

THE VOYAGE TO ILLYRIA

Not even interminable repetition can wear out the beauty of that passage, but Pericles' description of Marina shows a remarkable gain in profundity :

> Yet thou doest looke
> Like patience, gazing on Kings graues, and smiling
> Extremitie out of act.

Each passage is appropriate to its context, each creates exactly the right atmosphere, but the greater condensation of meaning in the last quotation is a measure of Shakespeare's development. Not only is it a perfect description of Marina, cramming into a single image all that she has endured, it also helps to create the vision of the play. Marina had to pass through the brothel, just as Pericles himself had to undergo a hell of grief and separation, not only to prove themselves, but to demonstrate that love, virtue, and constancy are triumphant over circumstance.

It is often assumed that the happy endings of Shakespeare's last plays are to be ascribed to the fashion set by Beaumont and Fletcher, but it is clear that he was moving towards the plot of forgiveness and reconciliation long before their plays were written. Indeed, if the preference of the Court is to be relied on, Shakespeare's tragedies were still pre-eminent even when Beaumont and Fletcher were writing tragi-comedies of the type of *Philaster*. Moreover, if literary influence of this kind was at work, judging from *A King and No King*, where the character of Bessus is clearly derived from that of Falstaff, this influence was in a reverse direction.

Cymbeline is full of echoes of the poet's own work, and this is due, not to exhaustion, but to a desire to gather up

AFTER THE STORM

the strands of all his work, and knit them together in the pattern of his new vision. *Othello* is recalled throughout the story. Posthumus is deceived by another Italianate villain, and the description of Imogen in bed recalls, with its sepulchral imagery, Desdemona's death-scene :

> O sleepe, thou Ape of death, lye dull vpon her,
> And be her Sense but as a Monument,
> Thus in a Chappell lying.

The same scene, with its Tarquin references, recalls both *Macbeth* and *Lucrece*.

> Our *Tarquine* thus
> Did softly presse the Rushes, ere he waken'd
> The Chastitie he wounded.

The fatal bet of Posthumus recalls Collatine's boast of his wife's chastity, but Iago-Iachimo is disproved in the end, and Imogen's life is spared. Pisanio will not kill her, and the wicked step-mother's poison proves harmless. *Troilus and Cressida* is recalled twice in one act. Iachimo's description of how he obtained the bracelet is an echo of Cressida's fall.

> She stript it from her Arme : I see her yet :
> Her pretty Action, did out-sell her guift,
> And yet enrich'd it too : she gaue it me,
> And said, she priz'd it once.

Though Posthumus echoes Troilus's ' Thinke we had mothers ', Imogen is slandered.

THE VOYAGE TO ILLYRIA

Is there no way for Men to be, but Women
Must be halfe-workers ?

Like Cordelia, Imogen is

> punish'd for her Truth ; and vndergoes
> More Goddesse-like, then Wife-like ; such Assaults
> As would take in some Vertue.

Titus Andronicus is recalled by Iachimo :

> She hath bin reading late,
> The Tale of *Tereus*, heere the leaffe's turn'd downe
> Where *Philomele* gaue vp,

and by Cloten in Act III. The character of Julius Caesar
is mentioned by Posthumus :

> Our Countrymen
> Are men more order'd, then when *Iulius Cæsar*
> Smil'd at their lacke of skill,

and again by Lucius, who talks of

> *Iulius Cæsar* (whose remembrance yet
> Liues in mens eyes, and will to Ears and Tongues
> Be Theame, and hearing euer).

Cymbeline, too, speaks of Caesar's ambition. The queen's
description of England, in the same scene, echoes John of
Gaunt's famous speech in *Richard II*, and the happy out-

come of the plot is a new version of the vindication of Hero in *Much Ado about Nothing*.

Cleopatra is depicted on the walls of Imogen's chamber, Belarius leads a country life in the manner of *As You Like It*, and Imogen seeks food as Orlando had done, while, like so many of Shakespeare's heroines, she is disguised as a boy. As Fidele, she is described as the fair youth of the *Sonnets*.

> By Iupiter an Angell : or if not
> An earthly Paragon. Behold Diuinenesse
> No elder then a Boy . . .
>   Were you a woman, youth,
> I should woo hard, but be your Groome in honesty :
> I bid for you, as I do buy.

The poet is reviewing his past work, and sanctifying his memories with the holy water of his faith. In the first act, the word ' dedicate ' is still contaminated. Iachimo says :

> I dedicate my selfe to your sweet pleasure,

but, in a passage which Mr. Murry has apparently overlooked, the word is again used, and this time it is cleansed :

>   So Ile dye
> For thee (O *Imogen*) euen for whom my life
> Is euery breath, a death : and thus, vnknowne,
> Pittied, nor hated, to the face of perill
> My selfe Ile dedicate.

THE VOYAGE TO ILLYRIA

What has caused the change ? Posthumus has forgiven Imogen though he still believes her guilty. Shakespeare has forgiven Southampton. Posthumus even forgives Iachimo :

> Kneele not to me :
> The powre that I haue on you, is to spare you :
> The malice towards you, to forgiue you. Liue
> And deale with others better.

Imogen ' is alone the Arabian bird ' ; she is the incarnation of Shakespeare's ideal, but she possesses a greater complexity and a riper humanity than the other heroines of the Romances. To compare her with Greene's Dorothea, as several critics have done, is ludicrously shallow. They resemble one another only in the circumstances in which they are placed. Imogen is no Griselda. She has a spirit and a noble humanity which make Dorothea seem a mere puppet, and the spontaneity of her actions exhibits a quality far above the goodness of the copy-books.

In another respect, *Cymbeline* exhibits the progress of Shakespeare's development. The scene of Fidele's funeral is a magnificent expression of the poet's new attitude to death. The dirge needs no commentary. It is written by one who has fully accepted the fact of death, and in his very acceptance there is peace and beauty.

> Feare no more the heate o' th' Sun,
>   Nor the furious Winters rages,
> Thou thy worldly task hast don,
>   Home art gon, and tane thy wages.

AFTER THE STORM

Golden Lads, and Girles all must,
   As Chimney-Sweepers come to dust. . . .
Quiet consumation haue,
   And renowned be thy graue.

The jealousy theme recurs in *The Winters Tale*, and once again the innocent wife escapes death, to be restored to her husband after his sixteen-year repentance. Polixenes is reconciled to Leontes through the marriage of their children. The love of the children atones for the sins of the fathers. Perdita, whose name is significant, comes like Marina from the sea ; and music is the natural accompaniment of Hermione's resurrection. The jealousy of Leontes has not even the excuse of forged evidence, and this may possibly imply that the jealousy of the poet was baseless. The word ' dedication ', as Mr. Murry has observed, is now fully purged.[1] It is used in a wonderful passage describing Camillo's plan.

A Course more promising,
Then a wild dedication of your selues
To vnpath'd Waters, vndream'd Shores ; most certaine,
To Miseries enough.

[1] The Shakespearean parts of *Henry VIII*, *The Two Noble Kinsmen*, and *Cardenio* were presumably written in retirement to help his fellows and John Fletcher to keep up with the demand for new plays. In the two plays that survive intact, there are no passages that throw any fresh light on Shakespeare. There is only a repetition of the old themes in a weakened form. The trial-scene of Queen Katherine, for example, is a less powerful version of the trial of Hermione. Any detailed discussion of these plays is outside the purpose of this book.

THE VOYAGE TO ILLYRIA

The scene of the sheep-shearing feast is a reaffirmation of Shakespeare's belief in love. It contains poetry of which one dare say nothing, since nothing can do it justice. The flower passage, Florizel's vow ' I am heir to my affection ', and the description of his love are all perfect.

> When you speake (Sweet)
> I'ld haue you do it euer : When you sing,
> I'ld haue you buy, and sell so : so giue Almes,
> Pray so : and for the ord'ring your Affayres,
> To sing them too. When you do dance, I wish you
> A waue o'th Sea, that you might euer do
> Nothing but that : moue still, still so :
> And owne no other Function. Each your doing,
> (So singular, in each particular)
> Crownes what you are doing, in the present deeds,
> That all your Actes, are Queenes.

In the winter of 1610, Shakespeare, always intensely interested in sea-voyages, storms and shipwrecks, must have read one or more of the reports, ballads and pamphlets relating to Sir George Somers's wreck on the Bermudas, *A True Declaration of the Estate of the Colonie in Virginia*, Rich's *Newes from Virginia*, the *Lost Flocke Triumphant*, or Jourdan's *A Discouery of the Barmudas*, and these appear to have been the primary source of *The Tempest*. Mr. Robert Graves has convincingly argued that Shakespeare was also influenced by Isaiah xxix, and by 2 Peter iii. 7–13. The significant juxtaposition of ' Ariel ', ' spirit of divination ', and ' devouring fire ', together with the sentences which give expression to the idea of the overthrowing of the enemies of Shakespeare, the deniers of the Phoenix vision, provoked the supposition that the poet conceived this portion of *The Tempest* one evening in December, when he heard the chapter read in church. But Mr. Richmond Noble's book, *Shakespeare's Biblical Knowledge*, has so amply demonstrated the poet's close intimacy with the Bible that this assumption is unnecessary, especially as the Genevan version provides the closer parallels. There seem to be further echoes from James iv. 14, and from the chapters adjacent to Isaiah xxix. We have already drawn attention to the debt that Shakespeare owed to Golding's *Ovid* in this play, and it should be added that the Earl of Stirling's *Tragedy of Darius* provides a fairly easily recognizable hint for the famous speech, ' Our revels now are ended ' :

Let greatnesse of her glascie scepters vaunt ;
Not sceptours, no, but reeds, soone brus'd soone broken :
And let this worldlie pompe our wits inchant.
All fades, and scarcelie leaues behinde a token . . .
Those statelie Courts, those sky-encountring walles
Evanish all like vapours in the aire.

But we must turn from the new influences to the old. From 1598 onwards, as we have seen, the theme of betrayal had been ever-present in Shakespeare's mind and work, and the mention of twelve years in *The Tempest* is significant. Prospero tells his daughter :

Twelue yere since (*Miranda*) twelue yere since
Thy father was the Duke of *Millaine* and
A Prince of power,

and this period corresponds with the duration of time since Southampton's betrayal. Now, in the calm after the tempest, the poet rounds off his work with this serene vision, in which the storm and stress of the Inferno comes only as an echo ' of old unhappy far-off things '. Though his ' wandring barke ' had been shipwrecked, he had survived. Well might he say with Ferdinand :

> Though the Seas threaten they are mercifull,
> I haue curs'd them without cause.

The tempest now was over :

> *Ioues* Lightning, the precursers
> O' th dreadfull Thunder-claps more momentarie
> And sight out-running were not ; the fire, and cracks
> Of sulphurous roaring, the most mighty *Neptune*
> Seeme to besiege, and make his bold waues tremble,
> Yea, his dread Trident shake.

Shakespeare could well ask,

> Who was so firme, so constant, that this coyle
> Would not infect his reason ?

But, in the plays since *Timon of Athens*, he had reviewed all the old problems in the light of the new vision : nothing now remained except to co-ordinate his final intuitions and depart in peace.

It will be necessary, first, to explain the symbolism of *The Tempest*. Shakespeare is not an allegorist in the usual sense of the word, and it is manifestly impossible to fix any one interpretation on all the characters. The play can be understood on many different levels. It may be read as a simple fairy story (the only possibility for the 'Impersonal' Critic), with the traditional Great Magician, Beautiful Maiden, Fairy Prince and Ugly Monster. The groundlings (if the play ever appeared in the public theatres) and the less intelligent courtiers would, no doubt, have seen no more in it than that. Others, perhaps, realized that the poet was saying farewell to the stage, though, if so, it took two hundred years for this suggestion to be revived by the poet Campbell.

Prospero is Shakespeare. Moulton and others have contended that since *Prospero* apparently means 'I make happy' and he behaves like God, he must be a god, and that the play is a parable of the workings of Providence in the world. There is no need to resolve this contradiction, but it could be resolved by saying that Shakespeare, in the Blakean sense, was in process of becoming divine.

Ariel is many things. He is, first of all, the genius of Shakespeare, which now longs, above all things, to be free. He is, also, the higher nature of mankind and opposed to Caliban, the lower nature or body, sensual and brutish : air and fire contrasted with earth and water. He is Love

a spirit all compact of fire,
Not grosse to sinke, but light, and will aspire.

He is, finally, a reincarnation of the Indian boy, the Southampton of the early days, the lovely boy of the *Sonnets*, the dynamic inspiration of Shakespeare's poetry.

THE VOYAGE TO ILLYRIA

Caliban (*Canibal* anagrammatized) has been interpreted as the noble savage dispossessed by the white man, as the Mob, and as the Missing Link. Another suggestion is that he represents the groundlings whom, at first, Shakespeare gave what they wanted :

> When thou cam'st first
> Thou stroakst me, & made much of me.

Later, the poet realized that if he did not wish to have his art ruined, he must keep Caliban prisoner. But Caliban is, more than anything, a symbol of ingratitude, especially the ingratitude that precipitated Shakespeare into the Inferno. Like Iago, Caliban is referred to as a demi-devil. Like Edmund, he is a lustful bastard. He is the mystery of iniquity, the Southampton of the betrayal.

> A Deuill, a borne-Deuill, on whose nature
> Nurture can neuer sticke : on whom my paines
> Humanely taken, all, all lost, quite lost,
> And, as with age, his body ouglier growes,
> So his minde cankers.

It is surely significant that Ariel groaned within the cloven pine for a time equal to that which had elapsed since Prospero had been cast out of his kingdom.

> Imprison'd, thou didst painefully remaine
> A dozen yeeres . . .
>   thy grones
> Did make wolues howle, and penetrate the breasts

AFTER THE STORM

Of euer-angry Beares ; it was a torment
To lay vpon the damn'd.

The cloven pine has been interpreted as the Drama, in which the spirit of poetry was imprisoned : but although it must be confessed that Shakespeare, on the evidence of the *Sonnets*, regretted, at times, the necessity of writing for the stage, it is impossible to believe that the author of the great tragedies did not guess something of their value, and the tasks that Ariel performed for Prospero were, presumably, the plays themselves. The imprisonment in the cloven pine must be the twelve-year inferno which the genius of Shakespeare had endured.

The three men of sin denounced by Ariel are the Machiavellian villains of the tragedies, now reduced to impotence, made subservient to Shakespeare's vision.

Sebastian cries :

Now I will beleeue
That there are Vnicornes : that in *Arabia*
There is one Tree, the Phœnix throne, one Phœnix
At this houre reigning there.

Prospero, after bringing his enemies into his power, forgives them at the prompting of Ariel, though it is clear that, all along, it had been his intention to do so, for, in the words spoken by Ariel, they are told :

Lingring perdition (worse then any death
Can be at once) shall step, by step attend
You, and your wayes, whose wraths to guard you from,

THE VOYAGE TO ILLYRIA

Which here, in this most desolate Isle, else fals
Vpon your heads, is nothing but hearts-sorrow,
And a cleere life ensuing.

Only the forgiveness of Caliban seems to come as an afterthought.

The kernel of the main motive of the play is contained
in the famous speech of Prospero, in which 'virtue' is
apparently used as the equivalent of 'forgiveness'.

Thogh with their high wrongs I am strook to th' quick,
Yet, with my nobler reason, gainst my furie
Doe I take part : the rarer Action is
In vertue, then in vengeance : they, being penitent,
The sole drift of my purpose doth extend
Not a frowne further.

Shakespeare has performed the rarer action because his
reason is now allied to his imagination. The actual forgiveness of Southampton had taken place in *Cymbeline*. The
Tempest owes its serenity to the fact that all its author's
problems were now solved, except the purely technical one
of bridging the gulf between two generations, while still
preserving an essential unity. Lytton Strachey's essay
on Shakespeare's last period cannot be taken seriously.
The evidence he brings forward to show that Shakespeare
was not 'serene' proves only that the poet was accepting
life and not escaping into a world of fantasy.

At the end of the play, there is a very strange epilogue,
which opens with a conventional appeal for applause, and
ends with a moving request for the prayers of the audience
on behalf of the poet himself.

AFTER THE STORM

                                    Now I want
       Spirits to enforce : Art to inchant,
       And my ending is despaire,
       Vnlesse I be relieu'd by praier
       Which pierces so, that it assaults
       Mercy it selfe, and frees all faults.
       As you from crimes would pardon'd be
       Let your Indulgence set me free.

Shakespeare is not saying with Tchehov ' Everything is forgiven, and it would be strange not to forgive'. He is
pleading, rather, ' I have forgiven those that trespassed
against me : pray, therefore, that I may be forgiven ; for
without my poetry I am an ordinary man with all the
frailties of humanity'.
    Prospero's closing words, ' Let your Indulgence set me
free ', express the other main theme of the play, the longing
for freedom which is expressed in the character of Ariel,
and by Prospero himself, and parodied in the conspiracy of
Caliban and his associates.

       No more dams I'le make for fish,
       Nor fetch in firing, at requiring,
       Nor scrape trenchering, nor wash dish,
       Ban' ban' Cacalyban
       Has a new Master, get a new Man.
   Freedome, high-day, high-day freedome, freedome high-
       day, freedome.

Ariel, at the beginning of the play, claims his promised
freedom, and Prospero is unreasonably angry at being
reminded of his promise. The text may well be disturbed

here, as the *New Cambridge* editors suggest, or the difficulty may be explained on A. C. Benson's theory that Ariel developed as Shakespeare wrote. A third possibility is that the poet, having determined to write no more after *Cymbeline*, was rebelling at the compulsion of his dæmon, or of the Court.

At the conclusion, Ariel is consigned to the elements of air and fire from which he sprang : he is free as mountain winds ; he lies in a cowslip's bell, flies after summer on a bat's back, or lives merrily under the blossom that hangs on the bough. Like Adonais, he is made one with Nature. Prospero himself, having finished his task by the conquest and forgiveness of his enemies, desires only to break his staff, and retire to Milan to meditate on death. Nor is it possible to doubt that both in Ariel's desire for freedom and in Prospero's several valedictions, we have Shakespeare's own farewell to the stage. Graves, at the poet's command, had waked their sleepers and let them forth. The long line of tragedies, symbolized by the mutinous winds, the dread-rattling thunder, and the war between the green sea and the azured vault had come to an end. At the conclusion of *A Midsummer Night's Dream*, Puck had begged the audience to :

> Thinke but this (and all is mended)
> That you haue but slumbred here,
> While these visions did appeare,
> And this weake and idle theame,
> No more yielding but a dreame.

In lines which may have been an afterthought in *The Tempest*, Shakespeare seems to refer to this earlier passage.

AFTER THE STORM

Our Reuels now are ended : These our actors,
(As I foretold you) were all Spirits, and
Are melted into Ayre, into thin Ayre, . . .
                our little life
Is rounded with a sleepe.

Not only is he describing the transitoriness of the earth
and of all that it contains, he is also implying the power
of his own dreams which, bodied forth in words, are as
lasting as the Earth itself.

        Forms more real than living man,
        Nurslings of immortality.

The theme of freedom is exemplified further in the love
of Ferdinand and Miranda.

        Might I but through my prison once a day
        Behold this Mayd : all corners else o' th' Earth
        Let liberty make vse of : space enough
        Haue I in such a prison.

This avowal by Ferdinand is closely followed by Prospero's
promise to Ariel, ' Thou shalt be free as mountain winds '.
Ferdinand gains his freedom by losing it. That this is not
a fanciful interpretation may be shown from a later scene
where the co-related ideas of freedom and slavery occur
repeatedly.

              Full many a Lady
      I haue ey'd with best regard, and many a time
      Th' harmony of their tongues, hath into bondage

Brought my too diligent eare . . .
The verie instant that I saw you, did
My heart flie to your seruice, there resides
To make me slaue to it, and for your sake
Am I this patient Logge-man.

Miranda echoes the same idea.

             To be your fellow
    You may denie me, but Ile be your seruant
    VVhether you will or no.
Ferd. My Mistris (deerest)
    And I thus humble euer.
Mir. My husband, then ?
Ferd. I, with a heart as willing
    As bondage ere of freedome.

Both Ferdinand and Miranda have found liberty in bondage
to each other. Love's service is perfect freedom.

    Shakespeare's conclusions on sexual love are a little
strained for us by his irritating insistence on prenuptial
chastity. Whether the betrothed, at whose festivities the
play was first given, had remained chaste or not, the con-
tinual harping on the same theme was insulting, and one
can only conclude that Shakespeare had personal reasons
for it. Berthelot has pointed out that the love of Ferdinand
and Miranda is stained with sensuality in Prospero's eyes,
and that this is purged only by the tests that they undergo.
' The union of his daughter with the son of his enemy is
an ideal compensation for the fatal love of *Romeo and
Juliet.* Friar Lawrence had warned them that violent

delights have violent ends.' This is true so far as it goes, but it is not a full explanation. For that, we have to go farther, to Ann's seduction of Shakespeare. They had given dalliance too much the rein, and barren hate, sour-eyed disdain and discord had bestrewn their bed with weeds so loathly. Suffolk, in 1 *Henry VI*, asked :

> For what is wedlocke forced ? but a Hell,
> An Age of discord and continuall strife.

Shakespeare's inability to connect love and sex had been overcome, at least temporarily, in *Antony and Cleopatra*. In the *Romances*, the heroines are all pure, and they emerge victorious. In the period of the Inferno, as we pointed out, the pure and constant woman was inevitably destroyed. In *The Tempest*, Shakespeare made his testament. He is convinced that women can be beautiful and true, and he is content to be the father of the pure woman. This is the origin of the moralizing of Prospero in the strain of Polonius and Laertes addressing Ophelia. To those who refer to the chastity of Isabella in *Measure for Measure* as 'rancid', Prospero's sentiments must come rather amiss, but a genera-tion, inclined to regard the marriage ceremony with less reverence, should at least remember that, to Shakespeare, marriage meant more than a legal undertaking.

Fidele was buried with his head to the East, for a reason unknown to his brothers. We have already indicated some of the evidence for considering *The Tempest* as the expression of an immortality myth. Just as, in so many of Shelley's poems written under the shadow of death, people pass through stormy seas, and arrive at an enchanted island, so Prospero and Miranda find sanctuary near the ' still vext

Bermoothes '. In these last plays, the symbolism begun in *Romeo and Juliet* and in Clarence's dream from *Richard III* reaches its culmination, and the new echoes of *Hero and Leander* which appear in the first two songs of Ariel, recall how Leander crossed the stormy Hellespont to gain the paradise—' the garden of the Hesperides '—of Hero's love. In Shakespearean symbolism, immortality and love are inseparable. It is not necessary to claim that he believed in a personal immortality. All we would say is that his imagination was led to invent or describe a posthumous paradise, but whether this was a poetical or an actual paradise, it is not the task of a literary critic to determine.

There is a tradition, emanating from the Reverend Richard Davies, Rector of Sapperton, that Shakespeare ' dyed a Papist '. It is possible, despite the fact that he was buried in Stratford parish church, but this is not to be pressed. The world of his last plays seems to be set in the pagan atmosphere of *King Lear*, yet, from this world, there emerges a system that is manifestly Christian, and this is all the more the impressive since it appears to have been built up on poetic rather than theological foundations. The evidence of his art leads us to believe that Shakespeare arrived at the Christian position by the process of his own natural development. *The Tempest*, therefore, is un-coloured by dogma. It is not a sermon. It is a parable.

The main ideas contained in it, of an overruling Providence, of forgiveness, of the transcending of righteousness and judgment, and the passing beyond good and evil, of the supreme importance of love and immortality, all these are the central teaching of Christ ; while the Crucifixion has its counterpart in the fate of the beautiful and the true in the great tragedies. Considered in isolation, *The Tempest* is a charming romance. Considered in its place in the canon, it is one of the surpassing achievements of the human mind.

Righteousness and peace have met together : mercy and truth have kissed each other.

In that, ultimately, lies the justification for this new study of Shakespeare.

✶   ✶   ✶

Wived inauspiciously, the seven lost years,
his dedication to a man right fair,
the worser spirit, the theft that love survived,
the dark betrayal, and the testament
in love's charred fragments written ; the descent
into Hell ; the breakdown ; sudden peace
after the storm, and Prospero's calm seas ;
life rounded with a sleep . . . Good friend, forbear.
And then the glory. Even judicial Ben,
answering adoration, himself adored :
' I loved the man, and do honour his memory
(this side idolatry) as much as any.'
What can we add to all the babble of praise
still rising to assail your deafened ears ?
Critics have plundered lexicons, and blown
their huge balloons of metaphor—to end
like the frog in the fable ; and your better path,
' Love, and be silent,' is untrodden still.

235

THE VOYAGE TO ILLYRIA

We laughed when you have laughed, and when you wept,
we were not far from tears.   We offer
you no praise.   But we have tried to understand,
and whether understanding's born of love,
or love of understanding, you best know.

APPENDIX

APPENDIX

SUCH a development[1] is better exemplified amongst composers than poets, and the nearest parallels are to be found in Beethoven and Mozart. The development of Beethoven has been charted in some detail. Until the third symphony (the Eroica), he believed in a morality of power, but in 1798 he had already begun to notice symptoms of deafness, and he was forced, as he said, in his 'twenty-eighth year to become a philosopher. It is less easy for the artist than for any one else'. Though obviously inspired by the example of Napoleon, the heroism bodied forth in the third symphony is Beethoven's own. Defiance of Fate, followed by the funeral of all hope, is expressed in the first and second movements, but from this despair there surged up a great flow of creative energy. That is the explanation of the last two movements. A large part of Beethoven's subsequent work is a restatement of the fundamental conflict of the Eroica, expressed in varying terms. It is self-evident in the Rasumovsky quartets, in the Appassionata, and in the fifth symphony. Sometimes the creative energy seems to rise from despair, sometimes from anguish and sorrow, sometimes from a superhuman wrestling with Fate. By the time the seventh symphony was written, victory had become habitual, and the tragic progress of the superb second movement is the expression of a conflict laid in the past. On the other hand, the finale is rather a triumphal march to the Promised Land than the rejoicings on arrival.

By 1810, Beethoven had mastered his experience. He

[1] See page 6.

THE VOYAGE TO ILLYRIA

had come to accept his deafness, and, on a certain level, he had achieved a state of balance. But his greatest adventure was to come. Between 1810 and 1817, his work was of relatively minor importance. His increasing deafness and consequent isolation, coupled with his growing realization that he could never marry, made him once again a prey to despair, and the mystical experience from which his later work sprang, followed a renewal of the old conflict on a deeper level of consciousness. This is the significance of the Hammerclavier Sonata and the posthumous quartets, in which we progress from a state of tension to a state of repose, from the storms and stresses of this earth to a brave new world, where all is forgiven, where all things are made new.

This experience was absolute, and though we know, from marginal notes to the scores of the last quartets, that he still had moments of despair, it is in these very quartets that he repeated and expanded the spiritual ecstasy of the last piano sonata. It is misleading to regard the *cavatina* of the B flat quartet as an expression of actual anguish. He had reached a state where sorrow and joy were facets of the same emotion. The *Missa Solemnis* is the religious affirm- ation made possible by this new experience. The opening movement of the A minor quartet, opus 132, is ostensibly a thankoffering composed during convalescence, but the patient is recovering in an alien country, almost as if risen from the dead.

We do not pretend that the development of Beethoven is exactly parallel to Shakespeare's. Their temperaments were widely dissimilar, and Beethoven never attained to the mellow humanity of the poet. He did not understand people, and he despised them. He lacked that ' comprehensive intelligence ' which most critics have perceived in Shakespeare. A dramatist is compelled to take all mankind for his province, but a composer, especially a deaf one, can shut himself off from his fellow men. We may draw attention, in this connexion, to Beethoven's growing unwillingness to plan his work within the capabilities of even the best performers. Shakespeare, in the gentleness and social grace to which his contemporaries bear abundant witness, was Beethoven's antithesis, but this makes the resemblances all the more striking.

A composer whose development is even more closely akin to Shakespeare's is Mozart. To a naturally balanced disposition was added a whimsical sense of humour, which warded off the worst horrors of the Inferno. To an inborn gift of lyric invention was joined a prodigious power of planning. A generous providence superadded not only the technical attainments of a virtuoso, both as a violinist and as a pianist, but a distinguished tradition of music, in his own family and in the ecclesiastical world in which he received his education. Fêted and petted as a child-prodigy by the most exalted personages of Europe, he was bound to suffer some diminution of Fortune's favour when he grew up. Differences with his father and quarrels with his patron occurred, and poverty and ill health took their toll.

The chastening effects of his misfortunes were reflected in his work, which began to outstrip the taste of the time. His harmonic audacities were taken for mistakes by his publishers, and *Don Giovanni*, the one opera of his that has never since fallen out of the world's repertoires, failed to please. A vicious circle—suffering, a fresh emotional advance, and the public's consequent failure to like or understand the work that displayed it, was set up. Pupils fell away. *La Clemenza di Tito*, a work commissioned to celebrate benevolent despotism, failed. From the spiritual night, there came a new dawn. *Die Zauberflöte* has suggested to more than one critic an emotional, if not actually a lineal affinity with *The Tempest*. The author of the libretto was probably Giesecke, who had previously translated *Hamlet* into German. Mozart's perception of the significance of the libretto cannot be in doubt. The man who had already composed the G minor symphony, and who was preparing his credo in the Requiem Mass, summoning his last ebbing flow of energy for the task, cannot have been orchestrating fairy-tales. The pathetic story of Mozart, humming faintly on his death-bed the Birdcatcher song, shows how near and dear to him was his last opera. The trials of the hero, the magic flute (the equivalent of Shakespeare's music), the Queen of Night, the joys of happy marriage, and the atmosphere of half-reality, with a double, treble, even quadruple stratum of symbolism, all these bring us to the confines of art and ethics, reminding us inevitably of *The Tempest*. In both, there is the music of the spheres.